D1567694

31078

DATE			
NOV 2 7 1985			
OCT 0 1 1988			
NOV 2 9 1989			
NOV 2 1 1990			
FEB 2 7 1991			
NOV 2 0 1992			

© THE BAKER & TAYLOR CO.

THE
CELEBRATION
BOOK
OF GREAT
AMERICAN
TRADITIONS

THE CELEBRATION BOOK OF GREAT AMERICAN TRADITIONS

BY WICKE CHAMBERS
& SPRING ASHER

Design Consultant
Chuck Clemens

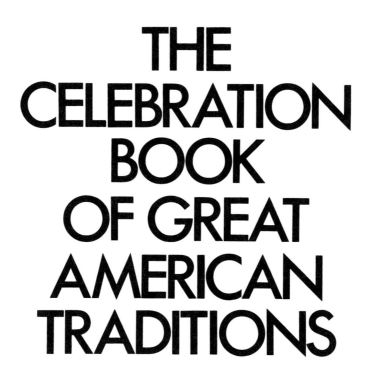

HARPER & ROW, PUBLISHERS, New York
Cambridge, Philadelphia, San Francisco, London,
Mexico City, São Paulo, Sydney

Grateful acknowledgment is made for permission to reprint:
     The artwork on pages 9, 61, 65, 77, 94, 123, 129, 130, 132, 161, 167, 184, 186, 187, 188, and 189 from *Food & Drink: A Pictorial Archive from Nineteenth-Century Sources,* by Jim Harter, Dover Publications, New York, 1979.
     The artwork on pages 63 and 69 from *Anne Orr's Charted Designs,* by Anne Orr, Dover Publications, New York, 1979.
     The photograph of Kelly LeBrock on page 41 by Richard Avedon. Courtesy *Vogue.* Copyright © 1981 by The Condé Nast Publications Inc.

FIRST EDITION

Library of Congress Cataloging in Publication Data

Chambers, Wicke.
  The celebration book of great American traditions.

  1. Holidays—United States. 2. United States—Social life and customs. 3. Family—United States—Folklore. I. Asher, Spring. II. Title.
GT4803.C44 1983   394.2′6973   82-48113
ISBN 0-06-015095-5

83 84 85 86 87 10 9 8 7 6 5 4 3 2 1

DEDICATION

To Bill and Helen Savitt and Jim and Peggy Oliver, our families whose traditions we've enjoyed, endured, and expanded with the Asher and Chambers clan. From Generation To Generation — Hallelujah!

Acknowledgements

Photography
Joe Benton

Copy Editor
Ann Evans Woodall

Typesetting
Alice Teeter

Layout
Carole Stowe
Tommy Westbrook

Typing
Margaret Chambers

Rubber Stamps
American Seal & Stamp
Atlanta, Georgia

CONTENTS

INTRODUCTION

From birthstones through milestones to tombstones life is loaded with traditions. Birthdays, graduations, weddings, Christmas, and Halloween are ancient traditions. How we design, renovate, update, and celebrate them is the focus of this book. *The Celebration Book of Great American Traditions* is a spirited guide for remodeling time-honored traditions with contemporary celebrations. It focuses on how people have recycled traditions to fit today's tastes and lifestyles.

Family traditions are like great old architecture. They, like brownstones houses, classic colonial structures, or early Williamsburg homes, offer strong foundations, good support systems, keep inherent cultural characteristics intact, and revolt against an assembly-line, ordinary lifestyle. They give life roots, history, continuity, and a distinctive character.

Be your own architect for the celebrations of life's moments and milestones.

CHANGING TIMES

Most traditions began as a form of worship; the celebration of a spring planting, a thanksgiving offering for a fall harvest, the rituals of fertility. Secular celebrations followed, changing the traditional holiday flavor from "Deck The Halls ..." to Deck the Malls.

Over the course of time, almost every holiday and traditional function of the family has passed out of the home and into the realm of institutions and professionals. As the T.V. ad says, "Who always takes care of you? If it's not your mother, it must be Howard Johnson." In almost every instance, from the making of clothes or the preparation of food, to the care of the sick or the rearing of children, there is a professional listed in the Yellow Pages who can handle the situation. Professionals can arrange flowers, but they can't provide roots or that sense of caring that a family or friends offer.

The way families celebrate traditions such as New Year's or a new job makes them unique. It gives a family its own particular (peculiar) personality and becomes a trademark that distinguishes one family from all others, including T.V.'s Cunninghams or the Brady Bunch.

THE GREAT AMERICAN TRADITIONS

Every immigrant who came to America carefully packed his roots and traditions along with his treasured possessions. St. Patrick's Day, spaghetti, and Bar Mitzvahs attest to that. Today most of the birth, wedding, holiday, and death traditions we celebrate have been stolen, borrowed or combined with those of other countries, religions, or ethnic groups. A little Irish lace and some fine French satin make the traditional American wedding dress. Traditions are made richer by this adoption and cross-pollination of ideas.

MOVING ON

Today, families are extended and made richer by adoption. Aunts, uncles, and cousins are usually home-grown, but in many instances they are adopted or chosen. A spouse is a relative you choose and so is someone who has "always been like a brother" to you or "the mother you never had." Second marriages create a new set of grandparents and new relatives who over the years will develop into a family who shares the same history. The mobile society has uprooted families as they moved to new jobs or new situations. The need for emotional support and for being connected causes people to join with friends to create this feeling of family. "Families" give support, a sense of security, and someone to help with the dishes after Thanksgiving.

Families are not the only things that have changed; so have traditions. They are constantly undergoing conversion, construction, adaptation, or abandonment. Families used to read *A Christmas Carol* together and have a special supper; now they watch the story together on T.V. and share a special McDonald's picnic. Being together is what counts. Some traditions are often abandoned with a sense of relief; others are changed to keep up with the changing times, ages, or events in a family. Still others are reinforced to provide a stable link from generation to generation, a sense of continuity.

Traditions, like Thanksgiving or a birthday cake, provide a patterned routine, a familiar structure, but when ritual becomes too routine there are no rules to prohibit a change. Change the time of day of a celebration, substitute a pizza glowing with candles for a birthday cake, or add an extra guest who brings new light to the family circle.

Traditions signal a rite of passage, a sign of "work in progress." Traditions offer emotional support and self-esteem in times of transition. It is important to keep the sense of family reunions and of family structure for the ceremonies of graduations, Bar Mitvahs, or weddings and to borrow ideas from others for these celebrations.

Some family traditions have developed into family businesses. The word about Carolyn DeShazo's spun-sugar flowers on the family wedding cakes spread so quickly that she moved from tradition to trade. Louis Bassett, who started making ice cream behind his house in Salem, New Jersey, in 1861, would have been pleased to see the family business not only survive the Civil War, but prosper well over a century later in the capable hands of his great-granddaughter.

WARM FAMILY FEELINGS

Traditions, no matter how old, were once new. The aim of this book is to spark ideas for celebrating "family" traditions, new or old. It offers tips, hints, and how-to's for creative ways to celebrate the traditions of birth, death, or other PERSONAL FAMILY DAYS.

Included are ideas on how to celebrate annual days, THE CALENDAR DAYS, by having a "Souper" Bowl Celebration on New Year's Day, decorating the dog on Valentine's Day, or arranging a close encounter on Halloween.

RELIGIOUS HOLIDAYS offer inspirations for gathering the "family" together and passing the stories of the faith from generation to generation.

EVERYDAY TRADITIONS cover all of the other days of the year. They offer how-to's for making ordinary days extra-ordinary by hanging up homecoming banners after camp, putting "I love you" notes in a briefcase, or having winter picnics before the fire.

Most celebrations center around a meal. The tastes and smells of FAVORITE TRADITIONAL RECIPES are a memorable part of the festivities. Recipes for a Maine Seafood Dinner or Gaelic Coffee for St. Patrick's Day add flavor to traditions.

Personal contributions give this book life and document the fact that traditions are alive and thriving across this country. Traditions are a gift that wrap a family and friends up in one another. They are the stuff, the glue, that provides Warm Family Feelings.

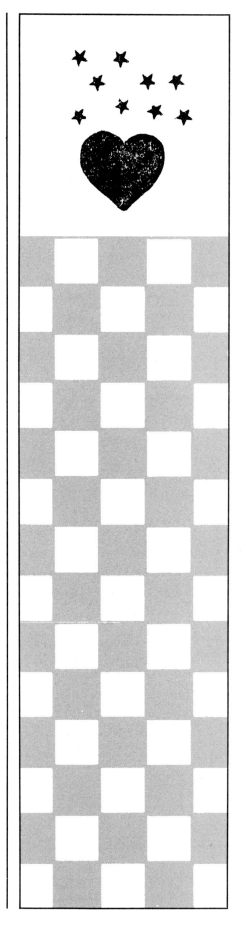

PERSONAL DAYS

Personal holidays are foundation-builders for family and friends. They inspire reunions and revelry. They include the traditions of new babies and new brides or grooms. They signal "Men/Women at Work" activities with the Coming of Age rituals of graduation, Bar Mitzvah, or debuts. Birthday bashes and banquets soften the awareness of the increasing "maintenance" that age and stage bring on.

Moving and funerals are the difficult days. Separations tug on the family security blanket and make the celebration of shared experiences and traditions more valuable. These reconstruction days can often pave the way to new beginnings.

Congregate and celebrate the traditions that keep family and friends constantly "under construction."

BIRTHS AND BABIES

A baby's birth rings up the curtain on a new generation. It heralds a fresh addition for a family and reestablishes its sense of continuity. Each new generation comes equipped with enough family characteristics to insure that relatives will remark, "She has eyes just like her mother," "He certainly did inherit John's smile," or "Well, you can tell he's a YOUNG!"

In large or small families, there's cause for rejoicing. There's a new relative to celebrate and new and old traditions that add major improvements to the family stock pile.

Taking note of a new twig on the family tree, naming, gifting, and gathering family history to pass along to this new addition call for a rebirth of some age-old traditions.

15

CELEBRATIONS OF BIRTH

A thousand well-wishers stood in the rain to welcome the news of the birth of Prince William of Wales. To the tune of an old soccer song, the crowd sang, "Nice one, Charlie, nice one son, nice one, Charlie, let's have another one!"

The welcoming fanfare for most new babies may not include such crowd-soaring fanfare, but it does call for some traditional celebrating. The following are some cork-poppers you might enjoy.

MAKING A GRAND ENTRANCE

Follow the royal tradition of posting the royal birth announcement on the palace gates. Post the announcement of the new arrival by putting pink or blue balloons on the mailbox or apartment door. Neighbors are usually well aware that the birth is imminent and welcome news of their new neighbor.

SHE'S GOT A NEW HEART FOB

When one grandmother started having a growing collection of grandbabies, her children began giving her antique silver hearts inscribed with each new baby's initials and birthdate. As the family grew, so did her collection of hearts. "It was the family tradition to start looking for an unusual antique heart as soon as the doctor told my wife the rabbit had flipped, or whatever it did," said one proud father.

AN INITIAL CELEBRATION

Tiffany gifts are a tradition in themselves in some families. They have been part of births, weddings, and great family moments for generations. For more than one hundred years, a Tiffany cup has been inscribed with the initials of each new male child in one family. With changing times this tradition may be altered to add female initials as young ladies demand their "place on the cup."

A BUDDING BEGINNING

Celebrate the birth of a new arrival by planting a flowering tree. In Switzerland an apple tree is planted for the birth of a boy and a pear tree for a girl. The tree with new roots, reaching toward the heights, weathering storms, and bearing fruit is an enduring symbol for a growing child.

CHRISTENING, BAPTISMS, AND BRIS

Nothing is as personal as a person's name. Besides having brown hair and brown eyes, a baby's family name is his first distinguishing mark of identity and the first tradition that is passed on to him. New babies often receive their "given" name and are welcomed into their religious communities at a baptism or a Bris, two of the most time-honored traditions. These services date back to earliest times and help to establish a child's religious identity. Cakes, clothes, and customs make this a family celebration to be treasured.

17

HIS "CHRISTIAN" NAME

The naming of a baby often takes place at a baptism. Through some weeping by parents and wailing by babies, the blessing of holy water during the service symbolizes making the baby a "Christian." This new name doesn't supplant the old, but is added to it. The term "christen" or "given name" comes from this age-old ritual.

When Prince Charles was christened, he was dressed in a robe of Honiton lace and white silk. It may have been elegant, but it was a hand-me-down. It has been worn by all of Queen Victoria's children, his own mother, and his aunt, and his son. Water from the River Jordan was used, in keeping with a custom that dates back to the Crusades.

EMBROIDERING ON THE EVENT

In one family a christening dress is passed from child to child. After the ceremony each child's initials are embroidered on the slip. It is a loving way for each baby to add his name to this family celebration.

A FIRST BOUQUET

A charming new baby girl was given a beautiful, small nosegay on her christening day by an older man who was almost five. This lovely, old-fashioned gift was pressed into her baby book as "her first bouquet!"

BABY TAKES THE CAKE

When the Brawleys, a nursery nurse and a pediatric resident, were married and working in the hospital, they were both impressed with the circumcision celebration and parties that were held when Jewish boys were born. "We decided that all babies were worthy of a party and a celebration, so when our first child, a girl, was born, we created our own celebration. A cake with 'Happy No Circumcision' written on the top and a bottle of wine were used for the celebration in the hospital. When our second child, another daughter, was born, we celebrated in the same way. Our next three children were boys, so we had a 'Happy Circumcision' cake along with our wine. We enjoyed helping our friends celebrate the births of their babies in the same way, and now we are passing the tradition along in the celebration of our three grand-children."

PLEASE PASS THE TRADITION

A Bris is a covenant between God and the Jewish people. It is symbolized by the act of circumcision. On the eighth day of a male child's life, it is customary to hold the Bris. A minyan, ten family members and friends, are invited to attend the ceremony. It can be held at the hospital, but it is more ceremonial at home. A Bris is also a naming ceremony. A special meal and grace are given afterwards. The service for a female child can also be held at home or in the temple or synagogue.

"With my first child I was nervous and apprehensive, but the service gave me such a strong sense of continuity and commitment that I can't imagine our family not sharing this ancient ritual together," a young mother commented.

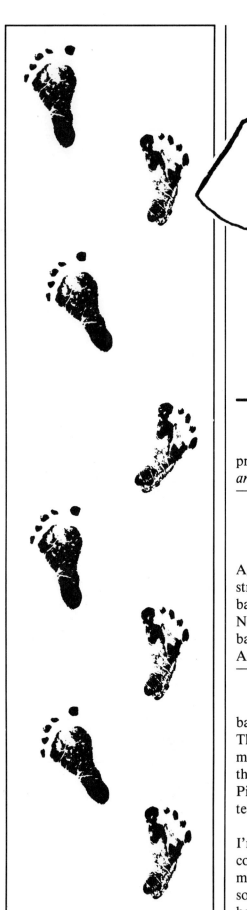

BABY GIFTS

Gold, frankincense and myrrh are perhaps the best known baby presents ever given. The tradition of giving gifts to celebrate the birth of *any* baby is an enduring and endearing one.

BIRTHSTONES
FOR THE FIRST MILESTONE

Birthstones are a longtime favorite gift. Fortune-tellers in the Middle Ages believed that they would influence the wearer's personality by strengthening the particular trait that the birthstone symbolized. July babies are given rubies to enhance their "contentment." Babies born in November receive a topaz to heighten their "fidelity." But April babies, with their characteristic "innocence," happily sing "Diamonds Are a Girl's Best Friend" when they receive their prized birthstone.

THE PREGNANT STORK

Baby gifts are given before as well as after the birth. An ad in a suburban newspaper read, "Pregnant Stork — Delivers Baby Shower Gifts." The ad had been placed by seventy-one-year-old Dorothy Rankin, who makes special costumes for all occasions. Not only did she give birth to the stork costume, but she also makes costumes for team mascots, a Pink Elephant costume, or a Crying Crocodile costume, complete with tears, for anyone who wants to deliver going-away gifts.

When asked if she wore the stork costume, she answered, "Oh, no! I'm only five feet tall, and I'd look like a platypus. I rent the white fur costume with a black top hat and bow tie to husbands and friends of the mother-to-be. They carry the bag of gifts at the shower and make a personal presentation. Babies are a special occasion, and I love my work because I think it gives the world a lot more fun on ALL occasions."

IN GOOD TASTE

One thoughtful friend had a bakery deliver to the hospital an incredibly delicious profiterole au chocolat cake decorated with a giant "Congratulations." This mouth-watering gift was sent home for the whole family to enjoy.

GLAD TIDINGS ON GLAD RAGS

A veteran parent brought gifts to the baby's older brother and sister that were a big hit. They were bright red T-shirts with "Mackenzie" and "Fiver" written in white on the front. On the back was written "Walker's Big Sister" or "Walker's Big Brother." Not only were they loved by the kids, but they served as a clever way of announcing the name of their new brother to their friends.

BALLYHOOING THE BABE

While Dad passes out cigars to his cronies to announce his new baby, older brothers and sisters can celebrate the event by passing out lollipops to their gang at recess. Everyone will enjoy sharing in the good news.

INCREDIBLE EDIBLE GIFTS

A baby food cookbook is an unusual gift for a mom who likes to "make her own."

A first-class way to toast a new arrival is with a bottle of cold champagne and a lobster dinner served to the proud parents in their hospital room.

A catered dinner at home on the night the nurse or a mother-in-law leaves is an endearing gift. "Nothing says lovin' like something from the oven," especially when it's beautifully prepared and served right at the height of a crisis.

The gift of a frozen main course or casserole, tagged "To Be Used When Needed," is just what any new parent needs.

WE SHOOT BABIES

A real memory-maker and family keepsake was the gift of a photographer who documented the baby's first homecoming. The pictures started with scenes of the baby in his hospital crib, shots of the doctor, nurses, and hospital friends. Shots of the new mother, her roommate, flowers, and gifts were also taken. The photographer followed the family into the car and snapped the welcoming party at home with the assembled grandparents and neighbors. The whole family got in on the gift and the memories.

RIDING IN STYLE

A unique gift was given by a friend who was a car nut. He borrowed a classic old Bentley to give the new baby and his parents a fabulous ride home from the hospital. "Nothing like making a happy occasion a classic one," the delighted new mom reminisced.

DATED GIFTS MARK THE OCCASION

Coins or stamps minted or printed in the year of the birth can be interesting gifts for a baby as well as the first entries in an exciting collection for his future.

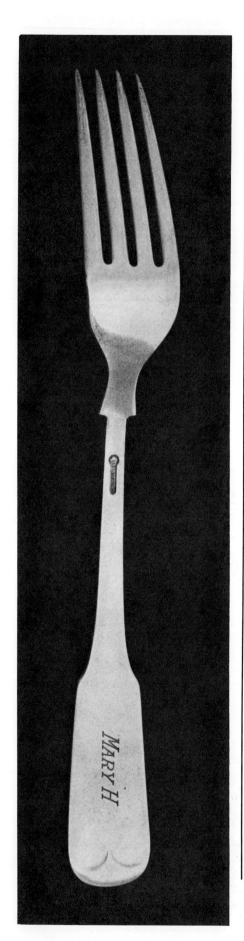

MARY H

Fine wine bottled in the year of the birth can become an even more special gift when it's put away to be opened on his eighteenth or nineteenth (depending on the drinking age in his state) birthday.

Newspapers dated the day of the birth are a wonderful souvenir gift. City magazines such as *New York* or *New West,* printed on the day or the week of the big event, make possible lifetime remembrances. It's fun for the "grown up" baby to look back on "his" times.

PROVIDING A FABULOUS RECORD ALBUM

Scrapbooks and baby books are hit albums in some families. Today most parents are so busy they don't have much time for "cut and paste" baby book projects. One inspired giver gives a "Memory Catch-All," a box (shirt box size) decorated with newspaper clippings, comics, the horoscope, and the T.V. schedule of the birth day. She adds, "It's a great storage bin for future pictures, first drawings, clippings, report cards, and souvenirs. At some later date when the life of the baby and the new parents is not so frantic, they can sit down together and cut and paste the items into a scrapbook. It's a fun way to reminisce." (Remind parents to date all materials and pictures.)

CULTIVATING A CLASS-CONSCIOUSNESS

A college jersey or pennant is a subtle gift for a boy or girl. Nothing like priming candidates early for a college decision, especially if the giver's college happens to be a rival of the parents' alma mater.

TO HIS CREDIT

Stocks are an early gift of ownership in corporate America. McDonald's, Atari, Loehmann's, and A.T.&T. are good choices for the future consumer.

A savings account, opened in the baby's name, with regular birthday additions is a gift that gets bigger and better.

GUESS WHO'S COMING TO DINNER?

When Hardwicke Oliver was born, family and friends gave her pieces of flat silver as gifts. To make the gifts more personal, her mother had the giver's name engraved on the back of each piece. Now when she sets her table, "Aunt Margaret," "Mrs. Shaw," "Judge Oliver," and others join the party.

WHAT'S IN A NAME?

Give a newborn a history of his/her name. It's a truly unique gift. A baby's name is his first most important possession. Almost all names have meanings. Early people were very aware of the various meanings of names and bestowed them with great thought. "John" in Hebrew means "gracious gift of Yahweh." Margaret in Latin means "pearl." Virginia pertains to spring. This is a gift with special meaning for anyone who receives it.

BABY HERITAGE

The birth of a baby means a new shoot on the family tree. Alex Haley tells the story of his own search for his family heritage in *Roots*. Millions of people not only have tuned in or have read his saga but have been inspired to begin a search of their own family's roots.

Jane Howard, in her book *Families,* comments that after stamp and coin collecting, genealogy has become the third most popular pastime. The median age for this new enthusiasm no longer belongs to the sixty-year-olds, but to twenty-year-olds.

FROM GENERATION TO GENERATION

The family tree acquires deep roots and many rings as it grows. Add two parents, four grandparents, eight great-grandparents, etc. for ten generations, and you come up with a crowd of 2,046 ancestors. One drop-out and you wouldn't be here.

It behooves a person not only to "begat" his link to the next generation, but also to keep up with all those who made his appearance possible.

Collecting personal family history can make for a good time and an intriguing adventure. Here are some rootsy suggestions:

★ Collect and reproduce family recipes.
★ Cut out pictures of advertisements, fashions, toys, or sports that represent the eras surrounding the births, marriages, or milestones of family members to make a family album.
★ Yearbooks, old family clothes, needlework, trophies, hats, report cards, or newspaper clippings make an interesting family "Show and Tell" exhibition.
★ Collect records of each era. Great-great grandparents who were married in the 1930s begat children who were married in the '50s, who begat children who were married in the '70s, who begat a baby born in the 1980s. The family's musical roots will include Gershwin, Elvis, the Beatles, and Punk/Funk. No one, however, will ever listen to music quite as loud as the new "begat" will.

BRANCHING OUT

Introduce your child to the family early. You may not have hallways filled with ancestral portraits, but thanks to Kodak you can cut out and paste together a mobile of your baby's "folks" for his crib. It has been documented that photographs in the crib increase a baby's intelligence.

Write to family members for a picture of their branch. It's a nice way of announcing your child's birth, especially if you haven't been keeping in touch. Put names with family faces as your baby begins to talk. A future family historian may be in the making.

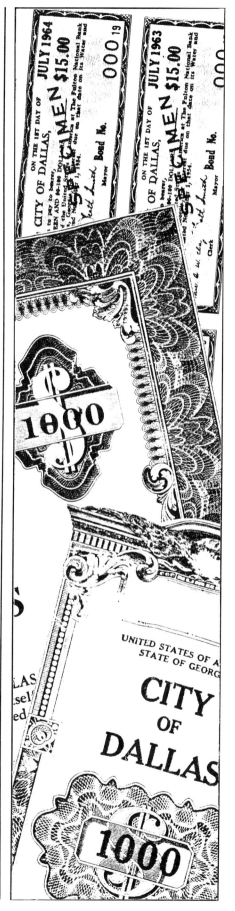

BIRTHDAYS

Birthdays are original, personal, noteworthy traditions. Some people like to forget them. Others like small celebrations, but for some the day has got to be a flag-waving, band-playing, joyous kind of merrymaking occasion.

Birthday celebrations began as a form of protection. As long ago as the early Egyptian days, people believed that a change in day-to-day life, like a birthday, opened the "door" to evil spirits. Friends and relatives gathered around with gifts and good cheer to keep the birthday celebrant from harm.

Today, birthday traditions include parties, cakes, gifts, songs, and celebrations intended to make each yearly add-on memorable.

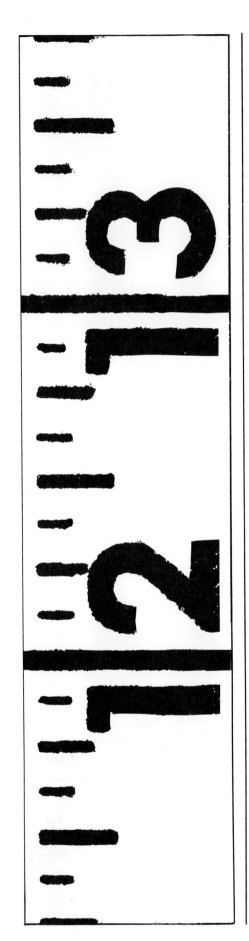

BIRTHDAY PARTIES

Turn on the spotlight and make way for the tradition of birthdays. Age and stage, moves and marriages change and alter the way this tradition is celebrated. The following party ideas for families, children, teens, and adults create memorable celebrations for this great tradition.

BIRTHDAY PARTIES
AGE 0-6 YEARS OLD

Birthday parties for babies are celebrations for proud parents. Later they turn into blowouts for growing babies. The following tips will help to make a young birthday party bright and bearable.

PRACTICAL PARTY POINTERS
FOR THE 0-6-YEAR-OLDS

★ Invite only one more guest than the age of the child (a one-year-old invites two friends).
★ Make the party short (1½ hours).
★ Take children home, if possible, as part of the party plan.

LESS IS BEST ... BUT

The Roman emperor Caligula arranged a little party for his daughter, Drusilla. He wanted a party in the tradition of an infant daughter of a great god, as he saw himself. There were two days of horse racing and a ritual slaughter of 800 beasts in the amphitheater of Taurus. Parents always make too much over first birthdays. So did he.

It is a tradition in the Wynn and Eric Henderson family on each first birthday to spread a sheet on the floor and to place the cake in the middle. The birthday child and his knee-walking friends are invited into the arena for a head-on, hands and knees, cake assault. Everyone, of course, is wearing his best Chocolate Soup finery.

For a slightly more civilized idea, try thumbtacking paper plates to a bench. The bench is the right height for this age and the plates won't fall on the floor. Party activities planned by one energetic, first-time mother featured six cardboard boxes with handles attached.

Each child sat in a box and rode around the floor, pulled by the parents. "It was a breathtaking occasion," she added.

A TABLE FOR TWO

Plan a small gathering of the birthday child and three little people, their "grown-ups," and possibly their grandparents. Arrange a table centerpiece of sand pails, dump trucks, or stuffed animals holding flowers or balloons. Provide bibs with names for the small guests (write with magic marker or embroider), and bring on the cake with three candles, one for each year and one to grow on. Don't forget the grown-ups. Cake and champagne make it an unforgettable occasion.

THREE'S COMPANY

At three, children begin to look with expectation toward their day. It is a good time to inaugurate a Birthday Tablecloth tradition. Start in the center and invite each guest to write his name. As the years go by, the handwriting improves and the circle expands.

If you can be outside, invite the three-year-olds to bring their trikes (to the park or your driveway). Decorate them with streamers and balloons. Ride in a parade and give bike horns for favors. Or in summer, ask guests to wear swim suits, turn on the sprinkler, and give blowing bubble stuff for favors.

LOOKING FOURWARD

Four-year-olds get into the spirit and love to help plan and prepare their party. Marguerite Kelly and Elisa Parson's in *The Mother's Almanac* recommend making ice cream flower pots. Fill flower pots with ice cream, top with grated chocolate (you grate, they assemble). Poke a hole with a skewer in the "dirt" and insert a straw with a flower top.

FIVE AND SIX PIN UP PICS

A five-year-old party can include a "Pin the Tail" with a difference. Instead of a donkey, get a large poster of Miss Piggy or a blow-up of the birthday child, and let the guests play "Pin the Nose on the Poster."

In winter, have a Fourth of July picnic on a blanket in front of the fireplace. Sand pail favors hold sandwiches and sodas.

In summer, try Christmas in July (or June or August). Get out the ornaments and decorate a plant, order a snow man cake, and serve hot chocolate with marshmallows.

GIVING UP IS HARD TO DO

Party hosts who are six-year-olds or younger enjoy opening each gift as it arrives. The giver has his moment of praise and recognition, even if giving up the gift is hard to do. Party favors soften the surrender. Instant party photos framed or unframed make fabulous flashbacks to take home.

IT'S IN THE BOOK

Birthday time is a good time to fill in a child's birthday book or scrapbook (p. 22). Tell him about "when he was little," how he got his name, and some celebrated "firsts." Put old photos and mementos of him in his birthday book.

IT'S ON TAPE

Jeanne Schmidt photographs each of her grandchildren "standing by a big yellow ruler that I have fastened to the bedroom door. After gluing the photo to the door, I also write in the height, weight, and age." Youngsters like hearing, "My how you've grown," when they've got the tape to prove it.

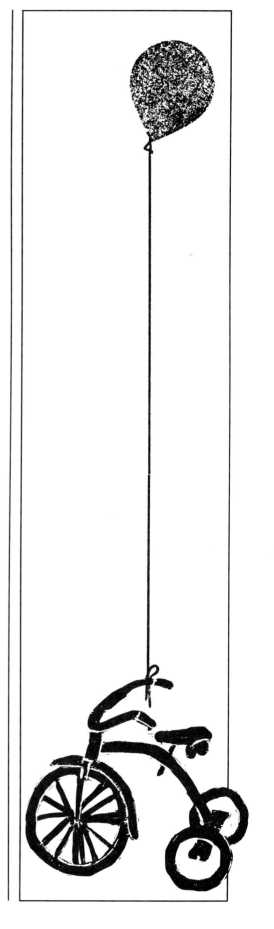

27

BIRTHDAY PARTIES
FOR A 6-12-YEAR-OLD

Six to twelve are the best birthday party years — not perfect, but controllable. Children like being able to be celebrated, some more than others. The famous movie director C.B. DeMille awoke at 6 o'clock on his sixth birthday. No one was up, and nothing had been done yet for this great day. He went outside, cut beautiful vines and greenery, and brought them home to decorate his "throne" in a way that was suitable for a "prince" on his day.

PRACTICAL PARTY POINTERS
FOR THE 6-12-YEAR-OLDS

★ Party plans and activities: Often birthdayers want to have the same kind of party their friends have had (the roller rink is a "tradition" one year, a certain magician another). It is important to have a lot to do, especially for boys. This sounds sexist, but try having eight eight-year-olds in your home and not keeping them busy. No, don't!

★ Guests: Fewer is best. Eight kids celebrating a seven-year-old will give the birthday child more attention than a crowd. When the guest list does grow see "They'll Do It All for You," p. 30.

★ Food: If it's more than cake and ice cream, consider your time and inclination. Hot dogs, pizza, or ingredients for "creating your own sandwiches" are acceptable and easily accessible for parents under pressure.

★ Date: Choose a time and a day that are convenient. Have a cake and a family celebration on the birthday and plan the party on a day that works best for both of you.

★ Hours: Shorter is always better. Parent pick-ups are always late.

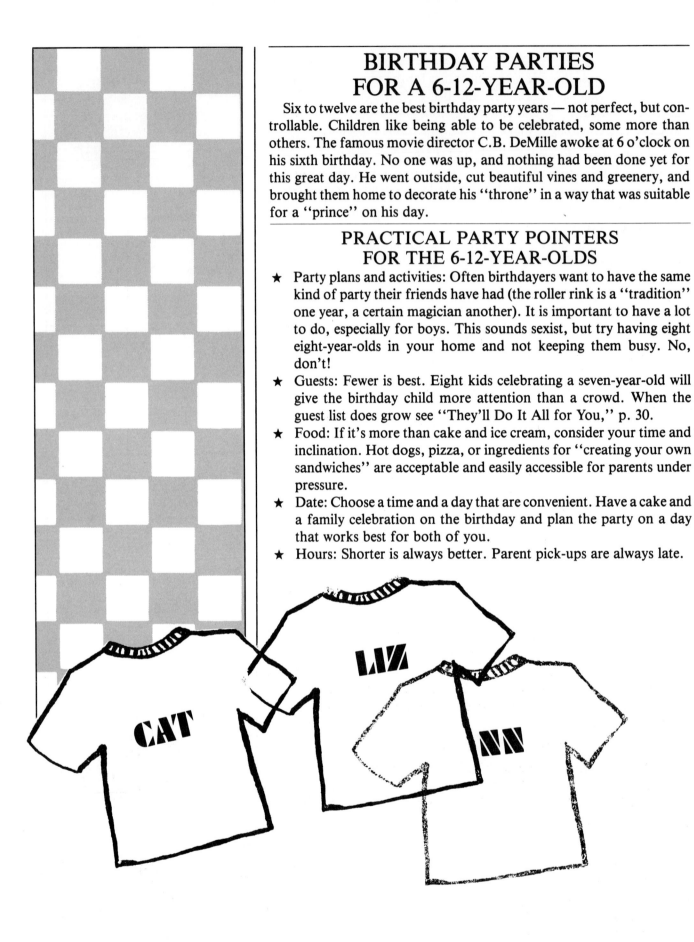

SPENDING THE NIGHT

Sisters Liz and Pam First have had the same birthday party every year for six years. Guests bring sleeping bags and pillows. Each one receives a large, white, man's T-shirt with her name written on the front with indelible magic markers or stencils that came from the hardware store. Everyone decorates her own shirt and then autographs the others. The party usually starts after dinner. Popcorn, music, talking and giggling pass the time from T-Shirt-Making until Make-Your-Own-Sundae time. The fixings for sundaes are set up in the kitchen: dishes, ice cream flavors, toppings, and spoons. (Make Your Own Sundae parties are great and easy for an "after-the-piano-recital" or "after-the-school-play-rehearsal" party for ages 7-17.) Then it is off to bed and more giggling. Breakfast is doughnuts and juice.

SPORTS IN THE PARK

Invite a group of kids for a picnic and a football, baseball, or soccer game. If you are giving the party alone, it is helpful to invite or hire a young person (17 or older) to help with the games. Write on the invitations: "If it rains we will go bowling at _____" (list alley).

Provide team shirts. Use white, men's T-shirts and put numbers on the back. Use red ink for one team, blue ink for the other. On the front, stencil giant initials of the birthday child in team colors.

DOING THEIR THING

Six to twelve are often the "specialization" years: dance lessons, swim team, soccer parties. You can use these interests for party ideas.

For a swimmer, have a swim party at the Y or at an outdoor pool.

Take a dancer and her friends to see a professional dance company perform. Circus acrobats are exciting to a crowd of gymnasts.

If your family is into camping and cooking-out, have a campfire, like Ann Samuels did. Roast hot dogs and marshmallows and tell scary stories (libraries have books of them).

If the birthday crowd is into T.V., take them to an amusement park to ride the bumper cars and play "Dukes of Hazzard."

29

MAKING HIS MARK AT SCHOOL

Have a birthday party at school. Your kid becomes the hero(ine) who gives everyone a break that day. Call the teacher in advance (she needs to plan the time). Some schools will provide the party; if you can't be there, you need only send the supplies.

It is easiest to have a cake and candles for show and cup cakes and drinks to go. If games are in order, here are two guaranteed winners:

SHOE BOX SHUFFLE

Supplies: 2 shoe box bottoms for each team
        (6 or 7 players to a team)
        Very small paper bags (1 for each player and extras)

1. Divide the class into teams of 6-8.
2. Teams line up at the starting line.
3. Place a chair 12'-14' from each team.
4. Place bags (6-8) on each chair.
5. Player #1 steps into boxes at start, shuffles to chair, blows up bag, pops it, shuffles back. The next player enters the shoe boxes and repeats.

The winning team completes the action first.

PASS THE ORANGE

Supplies: 1 orange for each team

1. Same team set-up as previous game.
2. All players keep hands behind their backs.
3. First player puts orange under chin.
4. Player #1 passes orange to #2.
5. No hands; use necks and chins only.
6. If orange drops, the one who was passing it picks it up and starts over.

Winners get "gold" coins (chocolate wrapped in foil).

SHELF LIFE

It is nice to buy a book for the school library in honor of your child's birthday. Let him choose the book from the librarian's list. Some schools have bookplates that can be put in the books with the child's name and the year. If your school doesn't, start a new tradition. Have 100 bookplates "quick-copied" at a print shop and present bookplates and a bottle of rubber cement to the school. (Cost of this should be under ten dollars.) The child will love to see his name, and he will be leaving his mark on the school.

THEY'LL DO IT ALL FOR YOU

Twelve ways to avoid having a birthday party at home. Call ahead.

★ McDonald's ... They will supply napkins, favors, ice cream, and even playgrounds. You supply the cake. Early lunch time is a great party time for the 5 and under set. It avoids fatigue and the crowds. (Ages 3-5)

★ Fire Station ... Tour the station, climb on the engine, try on the helmets. Don't forget the camera. Invite the firemen to join in the cake and ice cream celebration. A traditional fourth birthday party spent at the fire station gives older siblings a chance to reminisce about "their" fourth birthdays. (Ages 4-7)

- ★ Dairy ... Take a tour, see the milking equipment and the maternity ward. The bakery is a similar possibility. Free samples. (Ages 4-7)
- ★ Auto plant ... No free samples, but very interesting, especially to boys over 8.
- ★ Bowling Alley, Ice-skating Rink, Roller Rink ... Most of these facilities offer special prices, games, and prizes for large crowds.
- ★ Arcade ... Have a PacMan and Pizza Party. Some arcades have "bargain booklets." Give each child 4-8 games, then it's off to the pizza parlor. (Ages 8-12)
- ★ Amusement Park. Take one friend and spend the day. (Ages 8-12)
- ★ Shopping Center or Ecology Scavenger Hunt ... Give each child a list and a bag. The hunt can take place in a park or, in case of rain, in a shopping center. The list includes: 6 bottle caps, 4 cans, 7 cigarette butts, 20 scraps of paper (no tearing), 3 pop tops (no going in trash cans), or autographs of a salesclerk or park attendant. The party ends at the ice cream parlor. Order an ice cream birthday cake ahead of time. (Ages 7-11)
- ★ Bike Rally ... Give directions for the party destination to each biking team (2 to a team). Example: "Go 3 blocks west. Turn right. Proceed by stop signs. Go south, etc." You can give the same or different directions to each team. Give bike ornaments or a backpack for prizes and lunch for all at the last stop. (Ages 10 up)
- ★ Mystery Trip...Go to a surprise place, from a movie to a mountain top, on a bus — public or private. Serve refreshments on the bus. (Ages 8 up)

TEEN BIRTHDAY PARTIES

The struggles of adolescence are legend. Is it tradition, ritual, or just inevitable? It is a time of "Breaking Away," trying to escape the bonds of family and tradition. It is time for the family to back off, but stay close. Having a perspective and a sense of humor helps.

The fact that nothing is "right" in the world of the thirteen to eighteen-year-old is intensified on this day that has been glorified, by his parents, as his special day. Although "nothing" is right, doing nothing, which is what they often request, is worse. Plan something. It will make the day pass and then you can get on to the next regular "not so good day."

Age and stage change traditions. If a tradition doesn't work in the teenage years, drop it.

It's an Asher family tradition to have cake and ice cream, balloons, paper plates, and presents for breakfast on birthdays. It is a wonderful way to start a birthday. It's a time when the whole family is together and the little kids don't have to wait all day to be celebrated. When teenager Hugh Asher went to boarding school, his mom requested that his cake, traditionally served at dinner at the school, be served at breakfast. He was fourteen and mortified. This tradition will surely reappear in the next generation, but for now it's in hibernation.

PRACTICAL POINTERS FOR TEENS

Most boys are happy with presents and a family cake and then a no-family party with tickets to a sporting event or a movie with friends. Girls usually will be satisfied with the same, but they also enjoy plan-

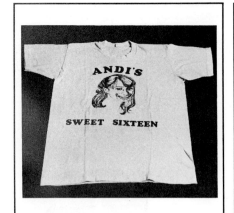

ning and having a party. All-girl parties are safer because, frankly, boys are not dependable guests at this age. They may show up, and if they do, who knows if their behavior will enhance the party. The best that can be hoped for at an all-girl party is that some boys will crash it.

Teens like to make plans for themselves or for their friends, and they don't need your suggestions. But just in case ...

FOOD FETES

Stage a kidnap breakfast. Wake up and pick up friends in pajamas. Bring them to the home of the birthday teen. Teens who drive can show up with doughnuts and orange juice or else prearrange with the birthday household to provide the breakfast.

Plan a moveable evening feast. Each friend prepares part of the party. Chips (hors d'oeuvres) at one house, dinner at another, and cake and ice cream at a third.

HARD ROCK PARTY

Teen Louis Franco invited the gang for a "Rock Concert" starring the Beatles. It was an evening of exclusively Beatles albums and ample refreshments. This is a great, spontaneous idea; but if you need invitations, paint "ROCK CONCERT... Artist, Date, Time, and Place" on small, smooth rocks with airplane paint.

SWEET SIXTEEN

Sweet sixteen parties are an old-fashioned idea, usually perpetrated by a mother who has had one. A luncheon given by mom for the girls is acceptable, and a sugar lump corsage is archaic but "so cute."

A more popular gift is a name collage. Teenager Connie Joel cuts out 5-inch construction-paper letters spelling out the name of a friend. She mounts them on a long, thin poster board and covers each letter with a collage of magazine words that describe the celebrant.

Artist Jackie Wolf had a caricature drawn of daughter Andi. It was printed on a yellow T-shirt and mailed with the invitation. It was a great surprise when the guests showed up at the party wearing them.

ASTROLOGY PARTIES

Foretell a fabulous future with an astrology party. Create wonderful horoscopes for all of the guests with a little help and humor from the book *You Were Born on a Rotten Day.* Have a positive-minded astrologer on hand to give out good thoughts and upbeat prophesies.

Writing in *Birthdays**, Linda Lewis describes a party given in California by a friend for his seventeen-year-old daughter:

> Mel's daughter is a Gemini and since Gemini is an air sign, her 17th birthday was full of floating things—kites, toy airplanes and helium-filled balloons. The balloons, released from the mountaintop where all the friends had gathered, each bore a stamped, addressed postcard to be returned to Jillene by distant finders.

Having a teens party on a mountaintop is a wonderful idea. It seems to symbolize the traditional struggle and the climb to adulthood.

*Birthdays: the delights, disappointments, past and present, worldly, astrological, and infamous.

33

ADULT BIRTHDAY PARTIES

The tradition of being surrounded by family and friends who protect you from evil on your birthday has great value for adults. Birthdays are milestones. Friends reinforce a sense of value, a feeling that "I'm loved," "people care."

DO-IT-YOURSELF HOLIDAY

If you are a birthday enthusiast, avoid disappointment by giving notice, not hints, to friends and family that your day is coming. Psychotherapist Dr. Gay Kahn recommends that you celebrate your day. "If you are at a time when there is no special someone to make a celebration for you, make your own. Invite people to lunch and/or dinner in honor of your day. Tell them it's your day. It is a great compliment to be invited to share a person's special day."

Harper and Row editor Larry Ashmead celebrates his Fourth of July birthday by sending out invitations to his "Annual 27th Birthday Party!"

INSTANT BIRTHDAY PARTIES

Birthday parties on the job create instant commotion, attention, recognition and guests.

Three of Sarah Richards' friends surprised her with a beautiful Baked Alaska aglow with birthday candles on her twentieth birthday as she busily worked behind the counter at Nantucket's The Blueberry Muffin. The customers, who were instantly part of the party, gave her a big round of applause and she treated them to a piece of the delicious Baked Alaska.

When nationally known book-buyer Faith Brunson celebrated a milestone birthday, friends turned up with a surprise birthday cake at

Larry Ashmead's
Annual 27th Birthday Party
Friday July 4th ○ 7 to 10 p.m.
Potato Road, Sagaponack

the Cafe on the Bridge at Rich's. Shoppers passing by offered smiles and congratulations and were given a slice of cake in exchange. Everyone enjoyed the spontaneous invitation to "celebrate."

THEME PARTIES

Themes add a little verve and a lot of conversation to a party. Phyliss Bronco is an art lover and shares her birthday, May 15, with artist Jasper Johns. For her day, she sent out Jasper Johns art postcards inviting friends for dinner in celebration of their mutual birthday. (Check a world almanac for your co-celebrants.)

When Australian-born Dorothy Hammerstein, widow of the lyricist Oscar Hammerstein, was "about" eighty years of age, she decided to give herself an Australian birthday party in her Park Avenue apartment. Nine Australian friends and relatives were invited for a traditional Tasmanian dinner. She declared that her day had begun with "a beautiful mornin'" and ended with "some enchanted evening."

THERE'S LIFE IN THE OLD GIRL (BOY) YET!

If you want to take the emphasis off of aging, a fun run, a family and friends baseball game, a party at an exercise studio, or a big bash at a roller-skating rink may be on target.

Deciding that a fortieth birthday should be fabulous, one aspiring hoofer planned a Tap Dance Luncheon. "The guests arrived looking much like girls in rehearsal clothes from 20th-Century Fox. The teacher was an old-time pro. In twenty minutes he taught the group a routine, and when husbands and lovers arrived it was "on with the show." Spinach salad, shrimp, strawberries, and wine followed. "So fine! No time to whine!" she boasted.

Another birthday enthusiast said, "I don't like to have people around me who fuss about age, so I invite people who never think about

Larry Ashmead's Annual 27th Birthday Party Saturday July 2nd ○ 7 to 10 p.m. Potato Road, Sagaponack

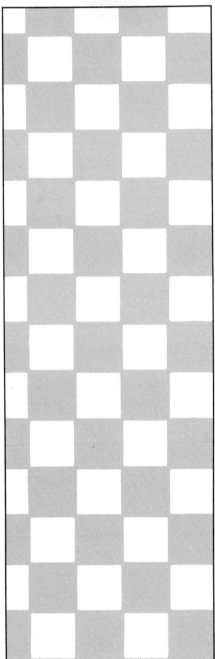

it. Teens! Every year on my birthday I ask each of my three teens to invite one or two of their friends for my birthday dinner. It makes them look forward to my big day. They always invite a friend who is funny, who will 'put out' to make it a fun night, and who is probably hungry for a good seafood pig-out. Traditionally, we go to Jarusek's for a wonderful messy seafood meal served on newspapers. The mess adds to the merriment and I never feel older—just fuller.''

THE GIFT OF SELF

Gift-giving on your birthday is a lovely tradition. Consider the man in the magazine advertisement who, on his birthday, sent the ''Cosmo Girl'' a bottle of champagne and his birth certificate with the message, ''I was born to be yours.''

One birthday female insures a happy birthday for herself by presenting her Annual (Secret) Anonymous Birthday Gift to someone else on her birthday. Recently, a friend looked out the window and saw her depositing a beautiful potted geranium on a neighbor's doorstep. The friend who witnessed the event promised to keep the secret, but she thought it was such a special tradition that she reported it in *Guideposts*!

AMONG FRIENDS

Celebrating a birthday gives friends and family a lift. It is a change of pace from the daily routine. One group of women takes turns playing ''super rich'' when one of the group has a birthday. On one birthday they may rent a limousine and go to lunch and to the theater. On another, they might have a day of beauty in a chic salon.

One husband planned a surprise slumber party for his wife, inviting her friends for a midnight champagne supper.

The same family who celebrated with ice cream and cake for breakfast invited some of ''Daddy's'' friends to join them on one of his ''big'' birthdays. When Dad came down at 7:00 a.m., they were all standing in the kitchen ready to launch him on ''his'' day.

Cinematographer Jim Collins picked up his special birthday lady in a limousine while a bus he had also hired picked up all of her friends. They met in style at the Steak 'n' Shake and had a fabulous parking lot party, with hamburgers alfresco.

The Supreme Court justices celebrate each other's birthday at a special luncheon.

Friends of Eleanor Roosevelt gathered each year at ''her'' bench at the U.N. Building to honor her birthday.

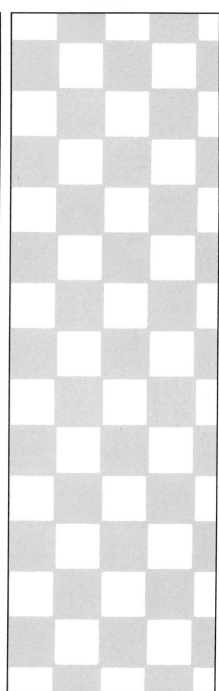

PARTIES OF THE TIMES

The *New York Times* found these celebrations newsworthy:

John Norwood Jr., an animator, and his sister, a writer, celebrated their joint birthday with a picnic ride back and forth on the Staten Island ferry with their thirteen guests. Background music was unexpectedly provided by two street musicians who were riding the ferry for the evening.

Why did the Norwoods decide to celebrate their mutual birthday on a ferry? "Because the ferry is romantic, enjoyable, wonderful, and has ample restrooms," Mr. Norwood said.

"And because he's cheap," his brother added.

Another "Party of the Times" featured architect Hugh Hardy, who shares his memorable birthday year with Radio City Music Hall, the Empire State Building, and the George Washington Bridge. He asked 300 guests for a cruise on a Circle Line boat around the city. The delicacies brought by the guests "were gobbled up even before the departure horn hooted."

GETTING INTO THE ACT

Many party ideas require some participation from the guests. Surprise parties require all the guests' participation in keeping the secret.

Invitations for Bill Anderson's party arrived in the form of bumper stickers. When the guests got to the party, each car had a sticker proclaiming, "Bill Anderson Is 50," firmly attached to its bumper.

Toasting and roasting the honoree inspires unusual participation. Guests arrived at one party with trophies, loving cups, an honorary degree, and blue ribbon badges celebrating the honoree as each person knew her best.

The invitation for a sixtieth birthday was sent out along with a piece from a puzzle. Each person brought his piece and a toast for the honoree to the party. As each guest made his toast, he added his piece to the puzzle board. When the ceremony was completed, so was the puzzle—a large, blown-up photo of the guest of honor.

ALTERNATIVE BIRTHDAYS

Squire Rushnell, Vice President of Long-Range Planning and Children's Programming for ABC, was born on Halloween. He loves it and as a kid felt that the fun and mischief was staged just for him.

Not everyone is so pleased. If your birthday falls on Christmas, during the summer when friends are away, or at some other time when the

occasion can be overlooked, find an alternative day on which to celebrate.

Consider the half-birthday and celebrate with a half a cake, or think about your lunar birthday.

Robert Louis Stevenson's daughter, Annie H. Ide, was born on Christmas Day. She wanted to have a day of her own. When she was fourteen, her father drew up a document giving her his birthday, November 13, as her own formal and legal birthday.

BIRTHDAY CAKES

The traditional birthday symbol is a wondrous cake aglow with candle power. The Greeks started it all. They stuck candles into honey cakes and presented them to the gods on festival days. But it was the Germans who made the first *geburstag torten,* and we've been gaining weight ever since.

CAKES THAT TAKE THE CAKE

Some families provide each celebrant with his/her favorite cake on his/her day. Pound cakes, caramel cakes, chocolate, coconut, and lemon cakes are popular favorites.

Patsy Maulvin of Rhodes Bakery in Atlanta says that cake decorations run in cycles. Television has a large influence. Smurfs are popular with all kids. Strawberry Shortcake creatures are popular with little girls. "Dukes of Hazzard" cakes and seasonal sports are always popular with little boys. Teenage girls know exactly what kind of decorations they like: anything purple, rainbows, and unicorns.

From ages four to forty, PacMan cakes are big. Big boys like bikini cakes, with or without the bikini! And a big-time guy loved his cake in the shape of a $100 bill with HIS picture on it.

Vogue's man of letters, Leo Lerman, was celebrated on his birthday with the ultimate in "good taste." — a stack of three books, each imprinted "The Life and Times of Leo Lerman." Each book was a different flavor — hazelnut, rum, mocha, Grand Marnier, and butter cream. The books were edited and designed by Bonte's in New York City.

EAT YOUR WORDS

Inscribing "Happy Birthday" across the cake goes back to the time when most people couldn't read or write. The written word was considered magic.

Phrases copied onto food, then eaten, were supposed to give the person the power of the thought.

Hattie Safter took this idea and created a birthday cake for her daughter's eighteenth birthday. The Hebrew number for eighteen is חי which means "life." It was the perfect food for thought for this special occasion. The presentation of the cake was followed by a spirited chorus of "To Life, To Life, Le Chaim," from "Fiddler on the Roof."

SUGAR-FREE LITE?

If you are on a sugar-free diet or just want to be chic, the following "cakes" have style. But if you are insistent on low-cal creations, fill a celery stalk with cream cheese, insert candles, and Think Thin.

★ Present a wheel of brie, or other round cheese, decorated with Kraft's squirt cheese and studded with candles.
★ Write "Happy Birthday" on a pizza with strips of green pepper. Add candles.
★ Serve a quiche with bacon bit inscriptions for a brunch.
★ Make a sandwich loaf filled with ham, chicken, and olive spread. Ice it with cream cheese and decorate with sliced olives, pimentos, or Kraft squirt cheese.
★ For a birthday drink with a twinkle, float candles in lemon slices in Sangria, champagne, or party punch.

NO-BAKE INSTANT CAKE

This family tradition started as a desperation/forgot-to-order the cake situation. Solution: go to the all-night grocery and get the following ingredients.

Large tub (round) or box of favorite ice cream
Spray-on decorative icing and/or candies
Jelly beans, candy corn, gumdrops (the colors of M&M's and red hots run.)
Mini-marshmallows
Chocolate wafer cookies, vanilla wafers, or animal crackers
Candles

Cut and remove ice cream container, leaving ice cream in its original shape. Place on cake plate and decorate with icing and candies. Use a simple candy design of H.B. for "Happy Birthday" and add the birthdayer's initials. Place cookies around the slightly softened sides and use mini-marshmallows or jelly beans as candle holders. Freeze until ready. (P.S. Frozen candles burn more slowly and evenly.)

IT'S THE REAL THING

Unfrosted layer cakes can be cut and designed in almost any shape. They are then iced to resemble the real thing. The family of a Coca-Cola lover presented him with a decorated Coca-Cola cake.

In Michael Rich's family, the birthday tradition includes a cake resembling the family car on the "driving" birthday.

A sport shoe cake of some sort will fit into the life of almost anyone.

CAKES BY MAIL FAIL

Families are not always together at birthday time. If someone in your family *always* had a chocolate birthday cake and you feel it's an annual tradition, then call a bakery in the celebrant's city. Ask them to deliver the cake and bill you. (This works!)

Make a giant chocolate chip cookie by cooking the batter in a pizza pan. Decorate and mail. If the cookie crumbles, it's still finger-lickin' good.

An entrepreneurial college student, with access to a mailing list of parents (through fraternities or clubs), could do a good business with a Birthday Cake Service.

FAKE CAKES
AND OTHER BIRTHDAY MISCHIEF

Candles that don't blow out—delight! They are available at some bakeries and novelty stores.

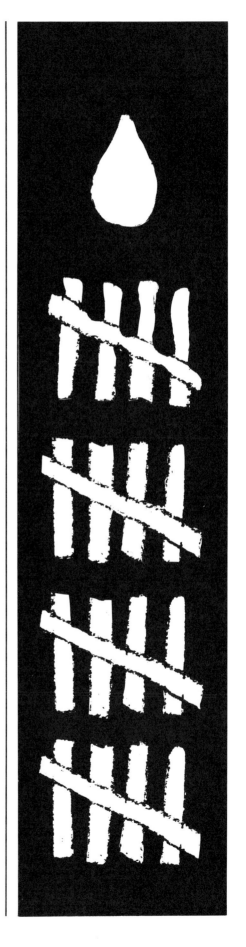

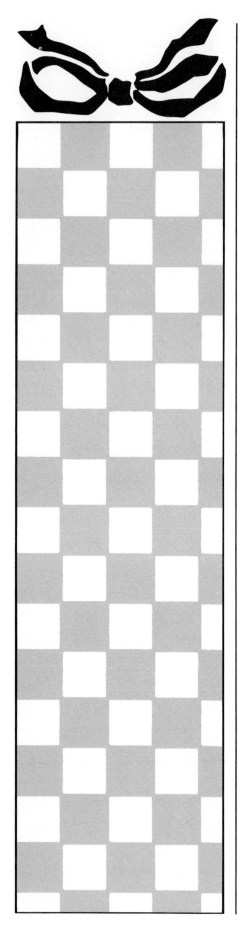

Fake cakes are crowd-pleasers. They are iced cake tins and can be given to major milestone celebrators, dieters, or birthdayers who lie about their age.

Ice a one-layer cake TIN (turned upside down) with great flourish and splendor. Present with plenty of fanfare and flaming candles, and then sit back and enjoy watching the honoree TRY to cut the cake. Fake Cakes are best eaten with tongue in cheek.

LIGHT UP YOUR LIFE

Candles on the cake are bound up in superstition. Peasants in medieval Europe lit candles on the cake as the birthday child woke and kept them lit all day, replacing the candles as necessary. The candles were meant to assure the celebrant's well-being.

Some families receive a large birthday candle as a gift for a newborn. Each year the candle is lit to burn down to the next mark for the next year.

In England, celebrants blow out the candles, make a wish, and cut the cake, but if the cake knife touches the plate, or if the celebrant speaks before finishing her slice, the wish will not come true. This sounds like a tradition adopted by a parent in need of a moment of silence!

BIRTHDAY GIFTS

Finding the perfect gift is an elusive bit of magic. In its place we give the "overboard gift," the "peer pressure gift," the "guilty gift," or the "gift you *know* he'll just love." But the "perfect gift" is the gift that gives a glow to the giver and the receiver.

THE BIRTHDAY BIRD

Dr. Seuss created a wonderful birthday story in his book *"Happy Birthday to You!* In it the Birthday Bird was the bearer of all birthday gifts. Because the book was a favorite of Harry, Louis, and Charles Elson, the birthday bird has become the traditional bearer of gifts on their day.

FABULOUS FIRSTS

An unusual bachelor friend sent McKenzie Brown a subscription to *Vogue* on her first birthday. "I loved it!" said her mother.

The late S.I. Newhouse had the same idea. He said that he bought Conde Nast Publications so he could give his wife, Mitzi, *Vogue* for her birthday.

On his daughter's first birthday, Prince Faisal sent her a rose for each of her first 365 days.

COMPLIMENTS OF THE HOUSE

Everyone needs attention and recognition. Birthdays are a wonderful time to "bombard" a person with an abundance of both. Sharon Strassfeld and Kathy Green suggest in *The Jewish Family Book* that each family member give the birthday person a compliment along with his gift. This ritual makes for an interesting sibling challenge that has produced such compliments as "You have great hair" or "I really like the way you draw spacemen."

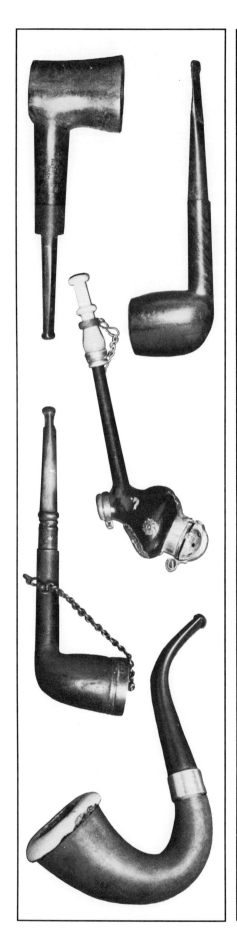

WHEN YOU WISH UPON A REFRIGERATOR

Everyone gets the "I wants." It is an affliction brought on by peer pressure and effective advertising. All ages are susceptible. One solution to this problem is the Family Wish List. When anyone in the family gets the "I wants," he or she writes the item on the Wish List posted on the refrigerator. Benefits from the Wish List are numerous: you never have to say "No" to a wish (no whining). The writer can do something about his wish (write it down). Checking the list provides gift ideas. When you write your wish, you recheck your old wishes, crossing off the things that you no longer "just have to have."

CATEGORIES

Some families divide presents in categories on gift-giving holidays. Categories include the big gift (from the Wish List), the money gift, the do-it-yourself gift, the useful gift (socks), and the nonsense gift.

SEND MONEY

Money gifts are always a hit. Send a dollar for every year (one of the benefits of getting older). Personalize a money gift:
★ Enclose a bill as a bookmark in a book.
★ Tie the bill in some crazy shoelaces.
★ Stuff money in a pair of gloves.
★ Carefully stick it inside the wrapper of a favorite candy bar.
★ Insert money in a balloon before blowing it up.

COLLECTIBLES

People who have collections give their friends a gift — the "gift" of knowing what to give them. Silver spoons, carpenter's tools, pearls and the ever-popular gold beads, art work and books are popular collectibles.

Commercial director Chuck Clemens collects models and cards and miniatures of the Empire State Building.

Photographer Lindsey Hopkins and his wife Wanda collect picture frames.

Interior designer Elice Schlesinger collects pigs. She gets wonderful presents from around the world.

Harper and Row editor Larry Ashmead collects twenty-three different things in all price ranges.

Do your friends and family a favor — start a collection.

MAKE IT MEMORABLE

Not everyone can give the gift of a handmade sweater, a quilt, or a stenciled tray. But a homegrown gift is memory-making, even if they only remember that it was a little lopsided.

★ Paint the giftee's name on anything: a coffee cup, a picture frame, a duffle bag (use stencil), an umbrella, or a door-sized mirror. Put a star over the name. Use airplane model paint.

★ Give a Birthday Coupon Book geared to the honoree's needs and your relationship to him. The man/woman in your life could use a shoe shine, a back rub, a home-cooked dinner for two, a car wash.

★ Make a pillow. Take a worn-out, too small, favorite T-shirt; turn it inside out and stitch together all of the openings except the neck. Turn it to the right side, stuff the shirt, and stitch the neck closed.

★ Create a pocketbook from favorite old blue jeans. Cut off the legs and stitch them closed. Add a rope belt, attach a handle to the belt loops, and decorate with acrylic paint, stitchery, or felt scraps and glue.

★ Catalog a record or tape collection. Make an alphabetical list of artists and number the records accordingly.

★ Assemble a group of favorite family recipes to give whenever a family gift is needed.

Choreographer Alvin Ailey created the truly memorable gift for his mother. Not long after he started his dance company, his mother came to New York for her birthday. He couldn't afford to shop for her at expensive stores, so he choreographed his now famous "Cry" ballet in her honor. Millions of mothers, brothers, sisters, friends, and dance lovers have long since enjoyed Mrs. Ailey's gift.

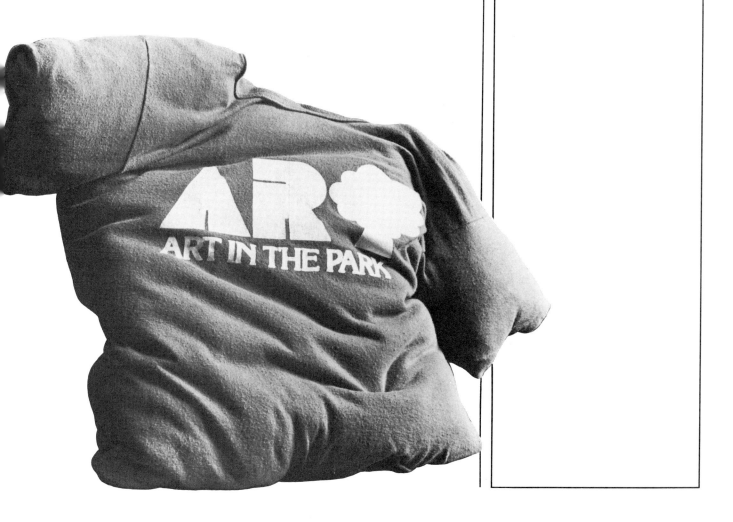

THE GIFT OF FREEDOM

Teens present a special "gift of giving" problem. Either they have their stereo, tape deck, clock radio, portable T.V., and a Gold American Express Card, or that's what they want.

One gift that you can give yourself and your teenager is the gift of freedom, a loosening of the reins. Realize that they are no longer children. Giving them freedom, and the responsibilities that go along with freedom, is often difficult, but it can improve a relationship. It is a gift that both will enjoy. For example, along with the family tradition that thirteen means having the freedom of no more "bedtime" goes the responsibility of getting oneself up in the morning or suffering the consequences of tardiness. Giving this gift is also giving the gift of trust. "I trust your ability to handle this freedom." Don't waiver, even when you KNOW they are going to be late.

THE GIFT OF CARING

Guidelines set by teens and parents give teens the assurance that parents care. They may bristle at the thought, but at least they don't feel neglected. Convincing them that these guidelines are a "gift" may bring on some interesting reactions.

★ Guidelines for New Drivers:

A driver's license is a major event for most teens. It represents the freedom to go on their own. Inexperienced drivers not only want to drive, but they usually want to take the gang along. The Morgans set up these guidelines:

1 passenger only in the car for the 1st month.
2 passengers only in the car for the 2nd month.
3 passengers only in the car for the 3rd month.

★ Guidelines for Check-In:

Kids can't always tell you where they are going to be every minute. In the Chambers family, kids must check-in between 5:00 and 6:00 p.m. so you know where they are. This should be reciprocal. They also like to know where you can be reached if necessary.

★ Guidelines for a Late Night Call:

The "You Can Count on Me" offer: Tell your teen that if she or he is in a bad situation, he can call you and you will come to pick him up, no questions asked. Then don't ask. It will usually come out anyway; and if you ask, who knows what he or she will answer.

Guidelines often give teens an "escape hatch" when they really don't want to participate. "I can't go. The old man at my house says 'No-go.' "

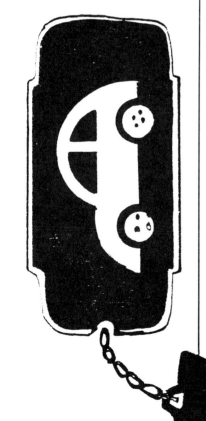

TAG ONE ON

Personalized gifts can bear many tags. The gift of a record entitled "A Little Help From My Friends" or "You Light Up My Life" can be tagged with a special thought: "This is Your Song for the Year."

One darling husband presented his wife with a new car and tagged it with a license plate that said "40." Didn't he read Robert Frost's definition of a diplomat — "a man who never forgets his wife's birthday, but never remembers her age?"

Friends of tennis player Dave Wolf took one of his well-worn, weather-beaten tennis shoes, painted it, and coated it with plastic. It was a personal paperweight with a note that said, "Your friendship is as comfortable as an old shoe."

Tag a birthday bottle of wine for a "little ol' wine lover" with a note that says, "This, too, was a very good year."

GIFTS TO GO

Helen Elsas keeps a gift supply shelf complete with scissors, tape, wrapping paper, and assorted gifts for young people. The stash includes flashlights, transistor radios, plastic label makers, and coupon books for ice cream and electronic game parlors.

THE GIFT OF TIME

The birthday tradition in the Brainoud family was to be invited to lunch or to the theater alone with dad. It was a special tradition for the whole family. As the family grew up, the tradition was altered. Now sister calls dad for lunch on his day or brother calls brother. The tradition created an awareness of the need for private times with individual members of the family.

For her ninetieth birthday Rose Kennedy wanted the gift of time from her grandchildren. She asked them to memorize and recite "The Midnight Ride of Paul Revere." They learned the poem and recited it — with mistakes — to see if she would notice. She did and lovingly corrected them.

Author and columnist Calvin Trillin and his wife Alice have given each other the gift of time. She started it by giving him "Cyprus" for his birthday. He has since give her "Iran." Says Trillin in describing the original gift in his book *Uncivil Liberties,*

> The task of being a well-informed citizen was a particularly onerous one when it comes to Cyprus. On the Cyprus question, I craved ignorance. I was tired of the Bishop. The history of Greek and Turkish settlement failed to fascinate me. Any analysis of the effect a Greek-Turkish conflict might have on NATO caused me to long for the Arts and Leisure Section ...
>
> "Don't give it another thought," Alice's birthday gift to me had said, printed in colorful letters on a map of the dried island. "Leave it to me ... You just tell me now at which point you care to be informed," Alice said. "I can let you know when it appears that they're going to start fighting again, for instance, or I can let you know. ..."

The perfect gift — information without excess copy.

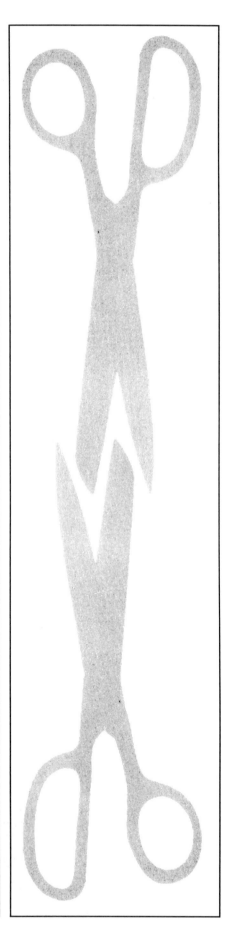

BALLOONS BY THE DOZEN

The balloon business is booming. Turn any day into a holiday — add a balloon.

★ Make invitations — Blow up a balloon half way and write the invitation on the balloon with bright magic markers. Deflate, enclose it in an envelope, and send it on its merry way.

★ Create place "cards" and favors — Blow up a balloon and write the name of guest on each. Tie one to each chair. Helium will make the balloons float happily above.

★ Extend a welcome — A bunch of balloons on the mailbox or on the apartment door signals a party in the making.

★ Decorate a table — Tie a bunch of balloons to the chandelier in the dining room. Balloon companies (see Balloons — Yellow Pages) have cans of helium for rent and balloons in special colors for sale. They will decorate and deliver a bouquet of balloons.

★ Make a centerpiece — Fill a basket with balloons. Fill the balloons with helium and anchor the strings to plastic "baggies" filled with sand or dirt. Put baggies into basket and hide them with colored tissue or flowers. Tie ribbon streamers to the balloons.

★ Decorate a mirror or a room — Rub balloons on your hair or wool carpet for a bit of magic. It will make the balloons stick to the mirrors or ceilings.

★ Make a celebration — Put a birthday flower in a clear balloon or fill a balloon with bits of confetti and pop it over the celebrant's head. Shower him with a rainbow of color. Decorate the bedroom door of the birthday person with balloons, streamers, and signs.

★ Play Smash & Crash — Tie a balloon on an 18″ string to each child's ankle. Indicate a circle. Contestants go into the circle and try to smash everyone else's balloon while trying to protect their own. The last player to survive with his balloon intact is the winner.

★ Play the Balloon Relay Game — Each team is given one balloon as the players line up. Player #1 places the balloon between legs and "hops" to a line (about 10 feet away) and returns. Then he passes the balloon to the next player — no hands. First team to make the round trip in record time wins. (For ages 8 to adult)

★ Stage a Water Bomb Battle — Fill balloons with water. Tie, toss, and take cover. Have a Balloon Shaving Contest. Blow up balloons. Spray with shaving cream. Shave carefully. No nicks, nice prize. (Use razors without blades.)

★ Send a Balloon in a Box — Fill a mylar balloon with helium and write a message in magic marker. Enclose in a box and mail. The helium will last two weeks in a mylar balloon. The recipient will get a rise out of it. (See Balloons in the Yellow Pages.)

★ Create a Balloon Business Card — Babysitter Happy Pottinger arrives at the home of a new client with a balloon for each charge. It is her trademark — a tradition with a treat.

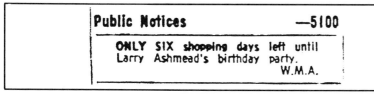

Public Notices   —5100

ONLY SIX shopping days left until Larry Ashmead's birthday party.
W.M.A.

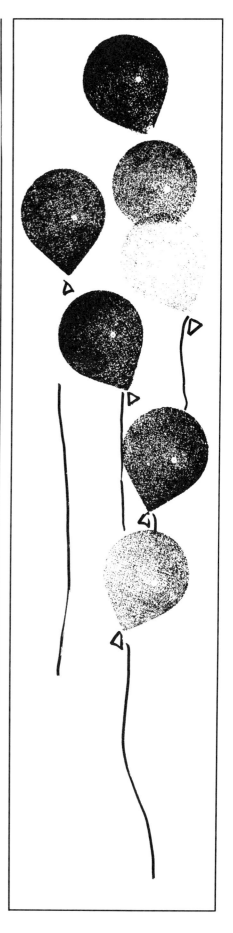

48

BIRTHDAY SONGS AND CARDS

Hear ye, hear ye! Birthday songs and cards originated with the tradition of open exclamation of the birthday in order to protect the celebrant. Greetings were delivered loud and clear early in the day to drive away evil spirits. Times have changed, but we are still proclaiming birthdays loud and clear. Billboards have proclaimed the day. Airplane trailers, loudspeakers at ball games, even garage sales signs posted on telephone street poles broadcast the fact that someone has reached another milestone.

Heralds of old have been replaced with crazy birthday-grams performed by costumed singers and dancers. Michelle Musolin was celebrated while instructing an exercise class. "Macho Man" entered with a singing striptease act that got her birthday off to a swinging start.

A SONG TO REMEMBER

Here is a story of a creative doctor's tradition: Linda Lewis, in her book *Birthdays,* describes the birthday of her daughter:

> When my first baby was born, at 4 o'clock on a warm June morning, I was wide awake, amazed, full of pride. "What's her name, what's her name?" the doctor asked. "Eliza," I whooped. Doctors and nurses, their mouths muffled in green masks, sang "Happy Birthday, dear Eliza" while I exulted. I tell her about it each year on her birthday ....

ROSES ARE RED, VIOLETS ARE BLUE, HERE'S A BIRTHDAY POEM JUST FOR YOU

Birthday poems go way back. If you are tired of the store-bought kind, make up your own or copy this one written by the Roman poet Martial in 66 A.D.

> Believing, hear what you deserve to hear;
> Your Birthday as my own to me is dear,
> Blest and distinguished days! Which we should prize.
> The first, the kindest bounty of the skies.
> But yours gives most; for mine did only lend
> Me to the world; Yours gave me a friend.

A SPECIAL DELIVERY

Penny and Jerry Goldwasser traditionally create homemade cards for family. These samples may inspire a birthday collage. The simplest card requires only cut-outs from magazines of words and pictures that remind you of the honoree. Paste these on a colored sheet of paper and you have a card that says they are the king or queen of your heart.

THE BIRTHDAY CONNECTION

Calling all fathers, mothers, sisters, brothers, and others. Today's families can be whole, split, near or far, but they can still stay in touch. Make a Birthday Connection. Telephone rates from 11:00 p.m. to 8:00 a.m. are low. Start the day with a ringing cheer for your birthday person.

COMING OF AGE

Graduations, Bar Mitzvahs, and debuts are coming-of-age rituals. These traditions mark a transition. They signal that major modifications in the original structure are being undertaken. There is a change in the graduate's identity, the Bar Mitzvah's role, the debutante's status. They've endured their conversion and marched off in the glow of family support with an unabashed grin. It is time to celebrate their labors with a toast, tears, and a smashing good time.

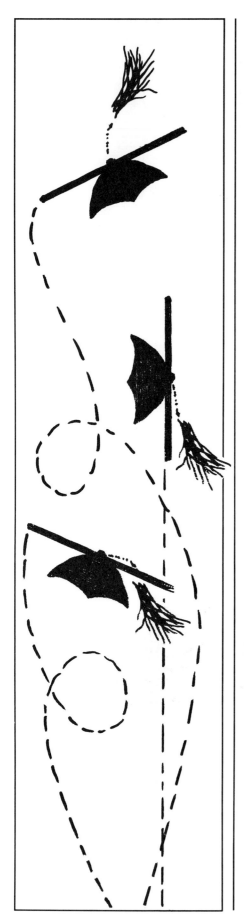

GRADUATIONS

Graduation is a timeless tradition complete with diplomas, caps and gowns, and yearbook autographs. It signals the end of a period of school work for the student and, happily, the end of at least one kind of tuition payments for the parents. Graduation is a time for pomp and celebrations.

WE'VE GRADUATED

The Driebe family had three graduates in the same year! Charles graduated from law school, Anne from college, and Elizabeth from high school. "It was quite a feat in itself just to make it to all those graduations," beamed their grandmother.

In honor of this achievement, the parents threw a big "We've Graduated Party." Over 200 of the graduates' friends from first grade to their present-day boy and girl friends attended.

There was beer, a band, and a beautiful big black and white cake with three capped and gowned figures on top. The cake proudly read, "Congraduations."

WITH HONORS

Graduation is a time of family recognition and pride. "There are five children in our family," said stylist Stan Milton. "It is our tradition that when each of us graduated from high school, our picture was hung on a special place on the wall. Getting your 'place' on the wall was an honor and an achievement."

YEARBOOK

Yearbooks are a tradition, but in the Childs family, theirs were unique. When each daughter graduated from high school, their mother, Lora, presented her with a scrapbook memento of *all* of their years. Their albums included letters from camp, pictures from special occasions, special notes from dad to daughter, birthday mementos, and pictures of friends. The book was bursting with magazine headlines and pictures that personalized their collections. After the first two graduates received their albums, they worked together on the last one. Each re-lived her coming of age on every page.

A DOUBLEHEADER

Alison Mazzola, daughter of John W. Mazzola, president of Lincoln Center, had a doubleheader excuse for throwing a coming of age celebration. She had recently graduated from Smith College and had landed her first job as associate beauty editor of *Town and Country*. She gave a Midsummer Night's Eve party with over 200 guests dressed in "fantasy costumes." The reality of any ritual calls for a fantasy fanfare.

A QUILT OF MANY MEMORIES

When Bobbie Carpenter's two daughters, Tracy and Libby, left their California home for college, they were wrapped in memories. For graduation Bobbie had made a patchwork quilt embroidered with special symbols for each of them.

Sneaking out of rehearsals for
Spring Fling with you was fun.

Hey Baby How's your
mocus. How does it feel to be
getting out? One more year for Paige
me. Have a good summer,
Alan

Nice Knowing you.... HAVE a good
Summer but it couldn't be as
good as mine.
Love ya,
Kim

This certificate here By indicates
that Joe Cardoza has signed This
Annual (sound familiar?)
AAAWW MARK!! Joe Cardoza.

If you weren't such
a hot you won't be you.
George Watley
It's been a
good year even
after English and
Capullavor. Good Luck;
Julie

CENTRAL

CHS

Hey Pitch. I'm writing th
How's it going? Stu in 20?
so you'll remember this annua
when you pick up this soft b
think of our great
Stu

In Graditude for the
Inquisitive mind +
e vocal student,
G. Sandler

LATER,
ARTHUR!

It's been great having you in
Algebra, English + Latin —
our favorite subjects. See
you next year when we'd be
Alpha Omegas together
Kathrine

I really did think
that you were drunk
at the dance!! Have
a great summer.
Luvi, Gera

WE'VE HAD FUN AND A GREAT YEAR DON'T FORGET
BIKE RIDING HOME ROOM YOUR RIGAT TEEL IS STRANGE
LOOKING BUT I LIKE SOMEONE ELSE NOW. SEE YA AND I

What a smash
What a laugh
stay'n your
lovin autograph
burp!

53

The idea came from another friend who made her daughter's clothes and had saved scraps from each masterpiece. When her daughter graduated, she used the scraps to create a many technicolored dream quilt for her.

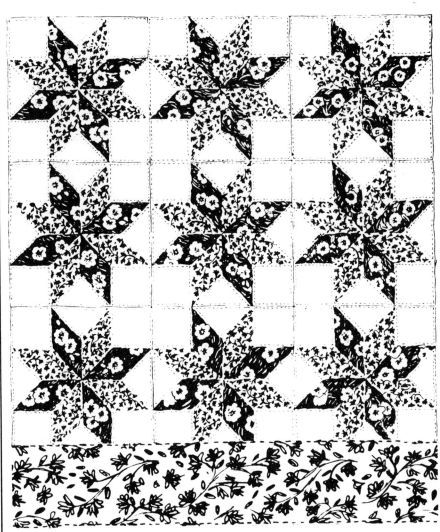

BAR MITZVAHS

A Bar Mitzvah (Bat Mitzvah for girls) is a traditional Jewish ceremony which not only signals to the congregation that a thirteen-year-old is ready to assume responsibility for his religious life, but also signals to his parents that he is ready to make his bid for adulthood as well.

Bar Mitzvahs, like other religious traditions, have undergone change. It is interesting to note that the Temple Emanu-El in New York City banned Bar Mitzvahs in the 1870s as too religious but reinstated the practice in the 1970s in response to the congregation's request for more traditions.

Bar Mitzvahs are family celebrations with friends and should be celebrated "at home," says Hattie Eisenberg in *Bar Mitzvahs with Ease,* "if your dwelling is larger than a walk-in closet and your family is smaller than the Chinese Army."

Family pride in this achievement, however, results in wall-to-wall people and elaborate celebrations. To quote Ms. Eisenberg, "Too much Bar and not enough Mitzvah takes away from the religious significance of this coming-of-age celebration."

PASSING THE FLAME

The Torah (scroll of the Old Testament) is a symbol of Judaism. It is the tradition at The Temple in Atlanta to pass the scroll from one generation to the next at the Bar Mitzvah. When the Torah is removed from the Ark, the grandfathers pass it to the father who then passes it to his son. It is a symbol of his accepting the responsibility of carrying his religious faith from "generation to generation. ..."

A FAMILY AFFAIR

Richard First's Bar Mitzvah was a family project. The entire family studied Hebrew together with a tutor for a year. Richard prepared his Torah reading and made a short speech at the service in appreciation of his family's support and participation. Each of his sisters said a prayer and opened the Ark, and his parents together sang the opening prayer. It was a very moving family affair celebrating Richard's religious coming of age. The guests gathered for a festive party at the Firsts' following the service in the beautiful chapel at Brandeis University.

WISH YOU WERE HERE

When Jason Gold made his Bar Mitzvah, he and his family decided to celebrate the occasion in Israel.

"It was a ceremony steeped in religious significance for all of us. The historical setting at the Wailing Wall added to the richness of the occasion, but there were trade-offs," added his mother Fay. "A completely unknown rabbi conducted the service and we missed the celebrating and merrymaking with family and friends afterwards. We wanted to escape all the hullabaloo and then we missed it!"

THE FAMILY TREE

Invitations are previews of coming attractions. They announce an event and request your presence.

Artist-grandmother Helen Asher designed the invitation for her grandson's Bar Mitzvah. Asher is the name of one of the twelve tribes of Israel. The family symbol is an olive tree. A beautiful paper tree was used on the invitation when Joey was Bar Mitzvahed. The inside of the card was handwritten and quick-copied. Other cards were left blank to be used as thank-you notes.

When Hugh was Bar Mitzvahed five years later, the family tree bloomed again.

PLANT AN IDEA

"Our synagogue did not have nice tablecloths. Rather than rent them, I bought yards of inexpensive, brightly colored fabric and made cloths that I later gave to the synagogue," writes Mae Shafter Rockland in *The Jewish Party Book*. Ms. Rockland also used white rose bushes instead of cut flowers for her son David's Bar Mitzvah. They planted some of the bushes at home and donated others to the synagogue garden — a fresh memory of his day of wine and roses.

DEBUTS

Debuts are a coming-of-age celebration for females. In most societies a young girl's initiation into womanhood comes at a time of menstruation. In today's society, the time that a young girl formally "comes of age" is determined more by age than stage and has plenty to do with "coming out" in style.

Parties are part of this coming-of-age ritual. Theme parties give guests a handle on the celebration. They are great icebreakers and give guests who don't know each other a common bond. As one guest put it, "It's easy to go up to a Red Tomato and start a conversation." Theme parties also give guests an opportunity to contribute to the making of a party in their own way. The following debut party ideas are super celebrations for any milestone.

SILVER SCREEN BALL

Invitations designed like a black and white filmstrip with pictures of favorite old movie scenes invited guests to dress in their Hollywood best. Costumes ranged from plain to fantastic. Blue-jeaned and leather-jacketed James Deans and heavily-sequined Mad Hatters rocked on the dance floor. Six hundred white and black helium-filled balloons burst out of film cans, and old lamp posts were hung with street signs that read "Sunset Boulevard" and "Miracle on 34th Street." Tables were filled with "The Godfather" pizza, "American Graffiti" hot dogs, "Sayonara" tempura, and "Breakfast at Tiffany" sweets. A "Born Yesterday" sign announced a continuing slide show of old movie clips interspersed with childhood pictures of each deb, her date, and her friends.

"Costume parties are fabulous. Everybody is on stage and That's Entertainment!"

OFF TO THE RACES

Dogwood Farm is a racing stable in middle Georgia. It was also the scene of a debut party that was a winner! Four busloads of guests arrived at the farm for an afternoon of blue jeans, beer trucks, square-dancing, and racing talk.

The most memorable part of the day was the naming of two year-lings. Each guest's name was put into a feedsack and then two slips were drawn. The filly was named for Catherine Cornett and the colt for John Mori. One guest, imitating a race announcer, gave a preview of a future Kentucky Derby Race. "And it's John Mori on the outside coming into the stretch, but it's Catherine Cornett, Catherine Cornett racing for the roses!"

CARNIVAL TIME

A carnival evokes a festive atmosphere. Big stuffed animal prizes make for an unstuffy party. Bright and splashy booths give guests the opportunity of winning prizes by shooting water guns at candles, knocking over pins with a softball, throwing darts at balloons, pitching bean bags into soft drink crates. The games are easy, the prizes are funny, and everybody is a winner.

SILVER SETTING

A lovely neighborhood lake provides the setting for this nostalgic party. Each guest was invited to dress in all white and to bring a dish in a silver bowl. The Gatsby-esque look of the guests gave the party its decorations. Buffet tables were covered with white cloths, silver candelabra, and white flowers. Quilts were spread for leisurely dining and a croquet set was close at hand. Tender was the night.

Premier: July 9, 1982

THE SILVER SCREEN BALL

STARRING

MARGARET CHAMBERS   HELEN MARGESON
KATHRYN DAVIS   LISA NEAL
SHERRILL LYBROOK   LEE ROOKER
MARY SCOTT KIRKPATRICK

WEDDINGS

Weddings are a love ritual. They are an ancient tradition that has flourished despite adversity, attitudes, and alimony payments.

Weddings not only bring two people together but are the ties that bind two families, cultures, religions, ethnic backgrounds, and often whole sets of children. The family tree undergoes instant growth as the newlyweds begin to blend "his" and "her" traditions into a single family unit.

The traditions of a wedding are age-old. Celebrating with music, flowers, food, finery, dancing, and parties with families and friends is as new and as exciting as you choose. A wide selection of bride's books and magazines assures that no two ceremonies will ever be the same. The following highlights focus on some touching or unique celebrations. Inspirations for Lovers and Anniversaries are also included.

ENGAGEMENTS

The use of a ring as an engagement token comes from the ancient custom of using a ring to seal any sacred or significant agreement.

An engagement ring is generally worn on the third finger of the left hand in the belief that the vein in that finger runs directly to the heart. Jewish wedding rings are worn on the first finger of the right hand for the same reason. If the truth be known, all veins on both hands run directly to the same important spot — the heart.

Valentine's and New Year's Eve are special times to get engaged. "One is romantic, the other represents a special beginning for the New Year."

WRITTEN IN THE SAND

Photographer Victor Smith became engaged at the beach. He secretly wrote "I love you. Will you marry me?" in the sand and then took his lovely lady for a memorable walk on the beach.

Once when another couple walked along the beach, they discovered a bottle half hidden in the sand. She rushed over to dig up the treasure he had so carefully buried. She uncorked the bottle and shook out the note and ring. The note said, "Will you marry me?" The ring said everything else.

IT'S IN THE BAG

When Atlanta Mayor Andrew Young was a college student returning home for the Christmas holiday, he was greeted by his special friend Jean. As he casually dropped his duffle bag on the floor, he mentioned, "By the way, your Christmas present is in there." She rustled through the sneakers and books until she found a very small box. "I didn't even unwrap it. I knew exactly what it was!" she said.

"Well, I was on my way to Washington to see this other girl ..," he said teasingly, but Jean made sure he never finished THAT story.

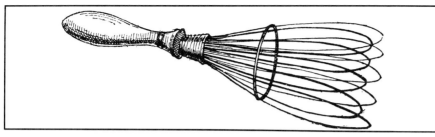

A SPLASH OF SHOWER IDEAS

Showers are a special way to launch a wedding. Whether they come as a drizzle or a downpour, they still provide the bride and groom with much needed household accessories and family and friends with a good excuse for a party.

★ AN HOUR SHOWER — Invitations designate the hour of the day or night for which the guest must bring a gift. If the invitation says to bring a gift for 7:00 a.m., try a snooze alarm, coffeepot, curling iron, shaving cream, or sexy lingerie for openers.

★ A ONE POUND SHOWER — Each guest brings a pound of "anything" from a pound of sugar, flour, cheese, meat, or coffee to a pound of pennies or a pound (16 oz.) of Scotch. If the couple are travelers, take them an English pound note; and if they're staying at home — and you are brave — try a puppy from the pound.

★ A PAPER SHOWER — Paper may be the gift suggestion for first anniversaries, but why wait? Start the couple off with a newspaper or magazine subscription, note pads, books, book plates, special sheet music, postcards, pen and ink drawing, cocktail napkins, or address labels.

★ A CHRISTMAS SHOWER — A first Christmas together can be special and a little sparse. Ornaments for the tree, wrapping paper and ribbon, hooks, scotch tape, mailing labels, tags, Christmas glasses or napkins will make their first Christmas seem more like home with gifts from family and friends.

★ A BAR SHOWER — A bar shower can include anything from wine, liquor, and bar accessories to little off-the-wall thoughts such as a bar of music, a bar of soap, or a crowbar. A gold bar may be a little too much for most pocketbooks.

★ A MR. CLEAN SHOWER — Clean up a couple's life with spray cans of Windex, scouring pads, oven cleaner, johnny mop brushes, brooms, soap, deodorant, nail brushes, or bubble bath.

If showers for the bride have reached downpour proportions, think of the guests' pocketbooks and plan a totally "idea rich — cost free" party.

★ A RECIPE SHOWER — One inspired hostess, who knew her guests were veterans in the kitchen, asked each to write down the recipe she used when she had only a "little time to make a big impression."

Family heirloom recipes are an inexpensive yet priceless gift. The thoughtful hostess supplies a recipe box, which also includes the menu and recipes from her shower, rehearsal dinner, and the wedding reception.

★ WEDDED BLISS OR A HELPFUL HOUSEHOLD HINT SHOWER — Mary Ellen doesn't have all the answers! This cost-

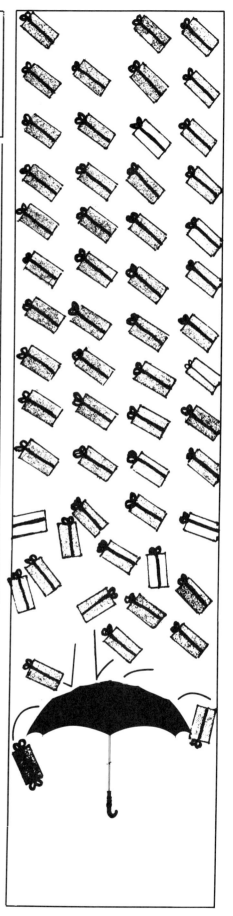

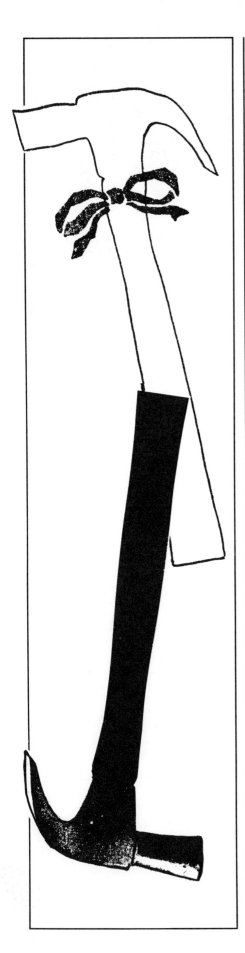

free party can include ideas from other husbands on how to get out of doing the dishes or cleaning the tub. Wives can offer helpful hints on how to get the groom to pick up his socks or put down the johnny lid. If the crowd is creative, the contributions for wedded bliss will range from romantic suggestions to how to handle weekend sports, car repairs, furniture touch-ups, T.V. tune-ups, hangovers, and sewing tricks.

★ A CHEAP THRILLS SHOWER — Freebie ideas for having fun for little or no money can be the basis for a fun party and can provide the couple, as well as the guests, with great ideas. Inspirations include a list of free concerts in the park, a library card, free films at the museum, a coupon good for swapping tapes with a friend who has a great collection, a list of early movies that offer cheap prices (take your own popcorn), or ballgames at home with hot dogs and beer.

★ Use the ribbons from shower presents to make a bouquet for the bride to carry at the rehearsal. Punch a hole in a paper plate and pull the streamers through to make a handle on the back. The bows make a bouquet that is a riot of color and memories.

THE GIFT OF GLITTER

Margaret Oliver was a master when it came to creating gifts with spray paint, glue, glitter, and fancy gold trim. It was her tradition to give the Bridesmaids' Luncheon, and her special gift was a Bride's Tool Chest. This was no ordinary chest. She took a fishing tackle box, spray-painted it, and lined the inside in matching white felt. Every tool or accessory from hammer and pliers to boxes of nails and picture hooks was sprayed white and decorated with rhinestones and glitter. It was quite a conversation piece, especially in one household when months later a repairman said to the bride, ''Hey lady, you got a hammer?''

WEDDING DRESS AND VEIL

''And the bride wore white'' is a popular concept, but not such an old tradition. The all-white, custom-made bridal dress became a tradition in the Victorian era. There was no such thing as a ''bridal dress'' before that. As far back as Roman times, rich, poor, and middle-class brides alike wore their ''best'' everyday dress and made it festive with ribbons, love-knots, laces, and flowers. Flowers have forever been the symbol of wedding celebrations.

HERE COMES THE BRIDE

When Alexandra Holden married, her grandmother, Lila Benton, nationally known owner of the Doll Hospital, made her wedding veil. Mrs. Benton uses fine antique laces and fabrics in restoring dolls, and the veil she created for Alexandra was magnificent. It was also the focal point for Alexandra, a paraplegic, as she came down the aisle. Her wheelchair had also been gloriously decorated with white ribbons and flowers laced into the spokes.

Hundreds of friends joined in the celebration and beamed happily at the end of the ceremony when the groom swept up the new Mrs. Ed Givens in his arms and carried her back down the aisle.

FLOWERS

LOVE IN BLOOM

Flowers are love in bloom. They brighten the day. They excite emotions and signal romance, beauty, and new life. Traditional flowers are used at weddings as symbols. Orange blossoms symbolize good luck, violets represent happiness, snowdrops offer hope, and roses and forget-me-nots are associated with love. Sweet smelling lilies-of-the-valley are THE wedding flower.

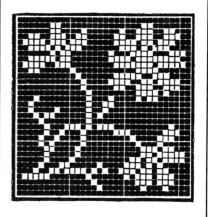

FAMILY FLOWERS

Floral designer Terry Alexander, owner of Very Terry, created the flowers for each of his three brothers' weddings. When his youngest brother married in a traditional Southern Garden Breakfast Wedding, Terry created a Victorian bouquet for the bride with something old, something new, something borrowed, something blue. An antique wedding bouquet-holder represented the old. A luscious variety of new, small white flowers was sprinkled with a few touches of blue. His mother's ring was borrowed and attached by a chain to the bouquet-holder. It was "Very Terry" and very traditional.

For another brother's bride, Terry recreated a Renaissance bouquet from Shakespeare's "The Taming of the Shrew." The bouquet for this second wedding had mixed greens, herbs, ivy and, as the song goes, "parsley, sage, rosemary and thyme."

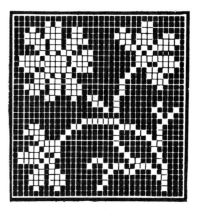

STYLED IN SILK

When wedding consultant Ann Nelson's three sons married, she created a lovely tradition for each of her daughters-in-law. In order to preserve their bridal bouquets, she recreated them in lovely silk flowers.

IN THE GARDEN

The daisies and sweet williams from one couple's wedding were replanted in the garden of their new home by the bride's parents. It was a wonderful surprise and a lovely keepsake.

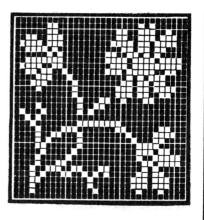

Potted flowers used to decorate the church or the reception on any occasion make meaningful gifts for family and friends. They can be replanted and are real "forget-me-nots."

RICE ROSES

When Jamie Jones married Rick Hurley in Tampa, Florida, her friends gave a party to make rice roses and mints for her reception. Early-comers cut strips of satin, sewed them by hand or on a portable machine, attached them to wire stems, and covered them with floral tape. Leaves were added and each rose was filled with rice. Young friends carried these glamorous rose baskets at the reception and gave one to every guest to shower the couple when they left. Rose flowers are an alternative to the traditional rice bags and are charming souvenirs for the wedding guests.

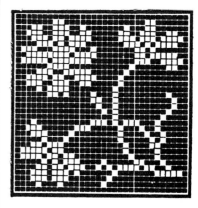

The children in the class taught by another bride made small bags of birdseed for the guests to throw at her wedding. The bride and the birds loved this shower of love.

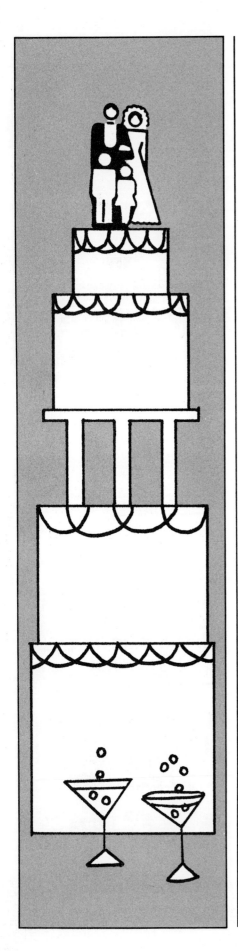

WEDDING CAKES

Every bride has sweet dreams of a special white wedding cake. Bakeries report that decorations for these cakes range from the traditional bride and groom, wedding bells or doves to fresh flowers and spun sugar candy flowers. Most cakes are basically pound cakes, but personal taste dictates the choice. Carrot cakes, French mocha, sponge cakes, and chocolate are used as long as they are decorated in the "here comes a wedding" style.

ELEGANT ENCORE

Floral designer Irving Gresham has created a second and third generation of unique wedding flowers. When he is asked to decorate a wedding cake with fresh flowers, he recreates the bride's bouquet. It is an innovative approach and provides a charming "close-up" of the original.

VISION OF SPUN SUGAR

When artist Carolyn Hassler DeShazo was married thirty years ago, she had a beautiful wedding cake decorated with delectable spun sugar flowers. The art of making these flowers was disappearing, so she found an expert to teach her the craft. She spent months refining and improving her technique. Finally, she could create sugar flowers that had the look of ribbon candy and the sheen of fine china.

"I started decorating the wedding cakes for my family. Later I did them for friends." Soon her tradition became her business.

She creates a nosegay arrangement with miniature spun sugar lilies of the valley, roses, and a mixture of the bride's favorite flowers. She does them in white or with a touch of color.

Carolyn also makes unusual wedding mints. She designs a large spun sugar cabbage rose as the centerpiece, and individual green mints shaped like rose leaves are arranged around the rose. Guests pick them with pleasure.

THE SECOND TIME AROUND

The second wedding cake for one couple, each of whom had children from a former marriage, was symbolic for both families. The cake was decorated not only with a bride and groom, but also with a figure representing each child.

TASTEFUL TIDINGS

When the bride, a CNN broadcaster, and her doctor groom married, they created a variation on a traditional wedding custom. Instead of having a receiving line, they cut and served one of TEN wedding cakes for each guest as they came up to speak. There were delicious choices of fudge marble, pineapple, coconut, and pumpkin cake or the Italian cream cake decorated as The Wedding Cake. While they cut the cakes, the bride and groom had time to have a personal visit with each guest.

THAT CUTS THE CAKE

Each child's birthday cake in Zaida Clay's family was cut with a special birthday knife. It became such a family tradition that when the first bride in the family made her wedding plans, she said, "I want the Birthday Knife to cut my cake." The birthday knife became part of a new family tradition.

A TOUCH OF CLOTH

Special cloths are often used to decorate the wedding cake table. Whether the cloth is one that was used at Grandmother's wedding or a lovely new one created by an aunt or godmother, it adds a special touch to the occasion.

FOOD FOR THOUGHT

Besides cake and mints, the wedding menu is very important. Hors d'oeuvres, a buffet, or a dinner offers a unique opportunity to serve traditional family foods or ethnic favorites. One couple requested their favorite foods be served at this, their first, most important party together.

MUSIC

Today's wedding music represents a variety of themes from the very traditional "Here Comes The Bride" to the contemporary "Love Story" or "Fiddler on the Roof."

Traditional or ethnic music adds a memorable note to weddings and receptions. Special love songs, old family favorites, popular theater pieces, or other themes relevant to the careers or lifestyles of the couple add to the festivity.

When Bendix chairman William Agee and Mary Cunningham married, they chose "The Impossible Dream," "I Think We Can Make It," and "We've Only Just Begun" for their reception.

At Jewish weddings, it is traditional to dance the Horah. Guests dance in a circle around the bride and groom, who are lifted up in chairs in the center of this spirited celebration.

THEY'RE PLAYING OUR SONG

Weddings can be personalized by the choice of special music for the attendants. The music for the bridesmaids in the wedding of a special couple who had just graduated from Davidson College was the graduation song of their alma mater.

In the wedding scene from the movie "Diner," the church was decorated in white and blue, the team colors of the groom's beloved Baltimore Colts, and the attendants walked to the Colts' fight song.

A JOYFUL NOISE

Music in the church can be played by musicians other than the organist. But no matter what the choice of music, nothing can be as splendid or as triumphant as a trumpet. Just before Cary Campbell and her father Cot walked down the aisle, a magnificent trumpet fanfare announced the wedding processional.

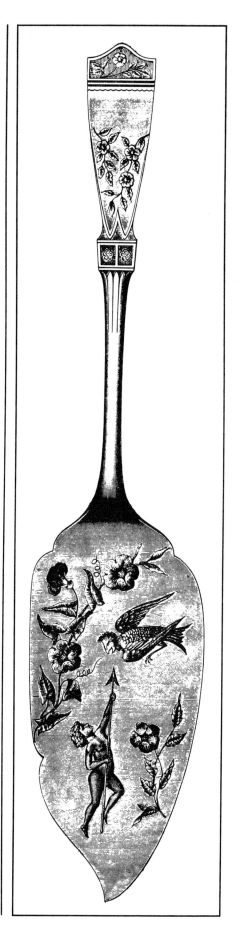

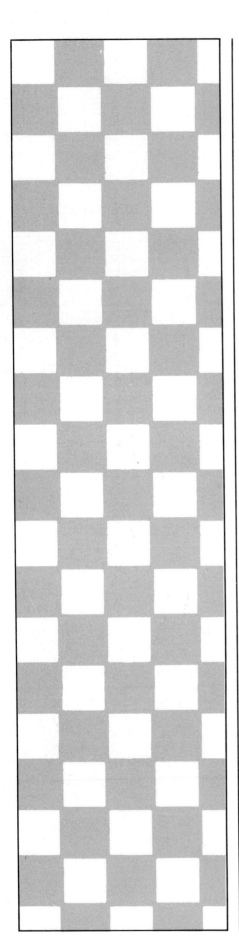

OH, HOW WE DANCED

Dancing at weddings is a spirited occasion. The dance floor becomes a marvelous melding of ages. Aunts dance with nephews, grandfathers with flower girls, "hopefuls" with the "barely interested."

To insure that this blending takes wing, ask the bridesmaids and groomsmen or chosen family members to start dancing and urge them to mix the ages of the dancing couples. Everyone, even those who have on their "sit-down shoes," gets "happy feet" at a wedding and should be asked to join in the celebration.

A REHEARSAL TO REMEMBER

Rehearsal dinners can range from the ordinary to the extraordinary. Here is one of note.

Janet and John Umhau used a theater theme for their son Andrew's rehearsal dinner. The invitation announced the preview of "Great Ex-

66

pectations.'' Place cards were made out of stars and a playbill program was at every seat. The cover of the program was designed with hit shows — ''I Do, I Do,'' ''Bells Are Ringing,'' and ''Ain't Misbehavin'.'' The Shakespearean menu listed the cast of characters. The scene-stealer was a five-minute slide show using pictures of the young couple to depict how the ''hero'' got the ''girl.''

SECOND WEDDINGS

Second weddings create new traditions. One-third of all weddings now are remarriages. Getting a new father or mother is not easy for a child. Even for those couples who are fortunate enough to get a rousing endorsement from the children, the bridal path may not always be strewn with rose petals. No matter how the wedding is to be celebrated, it is important that each child in the new family have the opportunity to participate and an invitation to do so. The following suggestions may help.

★ Include the children in the planning stage. No surprises. One ten-year-old son gave his mother away. In another wedding all the children stood up with their parents.

★ A honeymoon is a wonderful trip for the bride and groom. Make sure that the children stay with someone whom they will enjoy, too.

★ Traditions set up expectations. In one family, birthdays can be a big deal. In another, they may be just ''plain vanilla'' occasions. Parents in blended families should talk about how holidays, birthdays, and special days will be handled. Get the ''romance of anticipation'' and the ''reality of the event'' into focus.

FOR LOVERS ONLY
—OR—
HOW TO MAKE IT TO YOUR GOLDEN OLDIE ANNIVERSARY

Gannets are birds that live in Newfoundland. They mate for life, but each year they start their courtship ritual over again. It's called pair-bonding, and it's not just for the birds.

Romance is that magical ingredient that not only gets couples to the altar, but to their anniversaries as well. Good surprises, tender moments, appreciation, and interest can't be beat. Try some of the following inspirations and create your own.

FOOTBALL FANTASY

Joanna Woolfolk in her book, *Honeymoon For Life*, shows how she handled a husband who crawls in the T.V. set on the weekend with a six-pack. During a game between the Rams and the Bills, she said, ''Let's make a bet, no money, but the loser will have to do whatever the other wants for the rest of the day. You'll have complete control of my body for whatever purpose you want, or vice versa.''

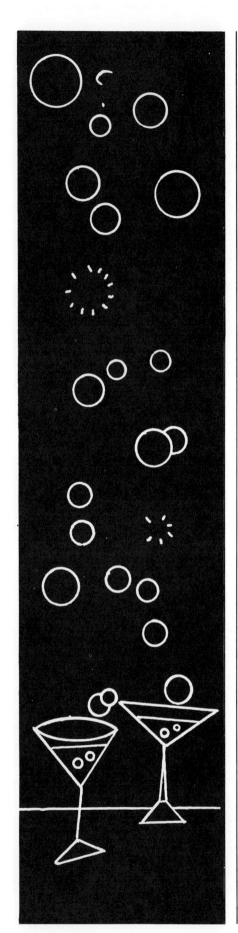

"That intrigued him. He won the bet and claimed his prize. I didn't feel like a loser," she added.

The next week she won the bet. It was a great pay-off.

Then during a dull game, he got so "turned on" just thinking about the bet that they agreed to claim the winner at half time.

"To tell you the truth, I've gotten to like football," she boasted.

LET'S PRETEND

During a Greyline sight-seeing tour of Charleston, South Carolina, the bus stopped at a flower stand. One husband of ten years got off the bus with the others, but when he got back on he had one rose for his bride-of-ten-years. Everybody on the bus smiled and, realizing their pleasure, his wife turned to the lady across the aisle and whispered, "We're honeymooning."

The word got around the bus, and soon people were taking their picture and offering them best wishes. "It was fun pretending to be honeymooners. We felt very special *and* very romantic."

TUESDAY PRESENTS

With one couple, if it's not a Christmas present or birthday present or an anniversary present, it must be a Tuesday present. Tuesday presents are "non-occasion gifts" that say "I love you." They can be anything from the gift of a new shirt to a candlelight dinner with "his favorites," to the gift of waiting while "her" car is being repaired. They don't happen every Tuesday or even on a Tuesday. They just happen to be "Attention-Givers."

DAY BY DAY

When life gets a little humdrum and you long for a little ah ha, realign your nightly routines like this couple does. She plans for Monday night, he plans for Tuesday and so on, each swapping the responsibility of designing large or small plans for the night.

"When it's my night, I'm in charge. I plan the meal and some small activity. I may not cook the meal, but at least I have to think it up. Then I plan a gin rummy challenge, get out the Scrabble board, or bring home two new paperbacks. The activity doesn't have to be time-consuming or expensive. It's the anticipation of the plans I create for her, or the ones she thinks up for me, that lets us both know we've been thinking about each other."

I GAVE AT THE OFFICE

It is the tradition of one couple who is happily intent on celebrating many anniversaries together "to have sex in our new office whenever either of us gets a new job." It is, psychologists say, a special form of bonding.

IT'S AN OLD SAYING

The tradition of saying "thank you," "please," "I really appreciate that (or you)," or "I love you" is probably the most important custom to hand down and spread around. These words show concern and appreciation. Every relationship needs a touch of that. Use daily for best results.

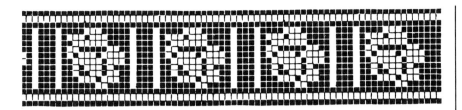

ANNIVERSARIES

Anniversaries are marvelous milestones. They call for a mini or major gift and celebration. The tenth, twenty-fifth, and fiftieth are the biggies.

For any special anniversary celebration, polish old silver baby cups, dents, bumps, and all, and use them as containers for flowers. Use baby bowls to hold matches and porridge cups as sugar bowls. It gives a special family glow to the occasion.

TIN ON THE TENTH

The traditional tenth anniversary gift is tin or aluminum. Not very glamorous for a very big milestone. To add a little allure to this anniversary, use any inspiration from champagne iced in a tin mop bucket, a tiny present dropped into a tin cup, or any gift from a sweater to a sable coat wrapped in tin (aluminum) foil.

A CLOTH OF MANY COLORS

Patchwork quilts made from a wild array of colors and patches each designed by a different friend, couple, or family member is a delightful and unique gift for any anniversary occasion. Friends of Deb and Bob First sent their guests an invitation with their patch included. They asked them to sew, embroider, draw, glue, or glitter a personal design on the patch and return. The host/hostess had the treasured pieces stitched together and presented the quilt at the party. It has become a lifetime keepsake which now hangs behind their bed.

HOW TO LIE
ABOUT YOUR ANNIVERSARY

Sona Holman and Lillian Friedman have written a wonderful book for nostalgia buffs called *How to Lie About Your Age*. It is filled with the events of each year from 1910 to 1969. It includes facts on scandals, Academy Awards, new products, fads, T.V. celebrities, world events, fashions, arts, and entertainment by the year.

Use this fact-filled, fun-time book to recreate the year of the wedding or the year when you'd like the wedding to have been. "Sirloin steak was 29¢ a pound" in 1934. In 1952 "chlorophyll chewing gum was introduced," and in 1969 "the American version of *Penthouse* magazine hit the stands." Tips like these spark memories and create inspirations for invitations, decorations, costumes, presents, or just plain fun.

A TEENAGE TREASURE

When the Jamie Goodes celebrated their twentieth wedding anniversary, they had four teenage children still at home. These four not only sent their parents out for "dinner on the town" at their expense, but

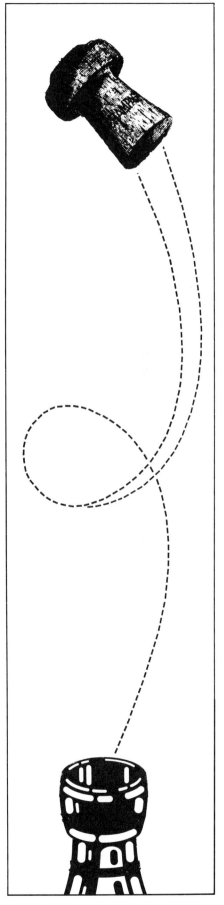

Frances Goldwasser

70

when the anniversary couple returned home that evening the house was filled with candlelight and soft music and EVERYBODY had moved out for the night!

They kept up this tradition every anniversary until the twenty-fifth. On this anniversary, the children feted their parents with a Surprise Party. Over one hundred guests from the book club, the tennis team, the office, and the church and friends from out-of-town showed up to join in the celebration.

PICTURE PERFECT

On their twenty-fifth anniversary, Helen and Joe Asher converted baby photos, pictures from friends' scrapbooks, and snapshots of their milestones into *Life* covers. These prized pictures were used as the invitation, and blow-ups of other "cover events" decorated the party.

At another special anniversary party, the table centerpieces were made with cylinders covered with pictures depicting favorite events in the couple's life. The cylinders were filled with a bright bouquet of flowers and became instant conversation pieces.

FABULOUS FIFTIETH

A fabulous fiftieth wedding anniversary calls for a fabulous celebration. It took one couple more than 800 invitations to include their children, grandchildren, and great-grandchildren, family members, their flower girl, and other members of the original wedding party to their fiftieth festivity. They had obviously made many friends together and separately over the years.

Dorothy and Lindsey Hopkins were married the same day as her brother and sister-in-law, Dr. and Mrs. Carter Smith. The newspaper's wedding photo of the foursome, decked out in hats and flapper fashions of the twenties, was used as the invitation for a joint fiftieth celebration. To the party, the fabulous, young-at-heart Dorothy wore gold lamé pants.

DIVORCE

No matter how special or significant weddings may be, they all may not last. There is a growing tradition of divorce. The following party suggestions speak to the brighter side of this event.

HER COMING OUT PARTY

A third-time divorcee gave herself a Coming Out Party after her divorce. It was a big event with many of the people she had met from all three marriages, wonderful food, and lots of spirits.

FREE AT LAST

A recent "court-appointed" bachelor was given a party after his divorce that was almost as large as his wedding reception. A banner hung over the cake that read "Free At Last," and the chocolate cake was decorated with a single figure with a fishing rod, a golf club, a tennis racquet, and every piece of sports equipment a bachelor could handle. The guests talked and mingled while the deejay played old favorites like "She Got the Gold Mine and I Got the Shaft."

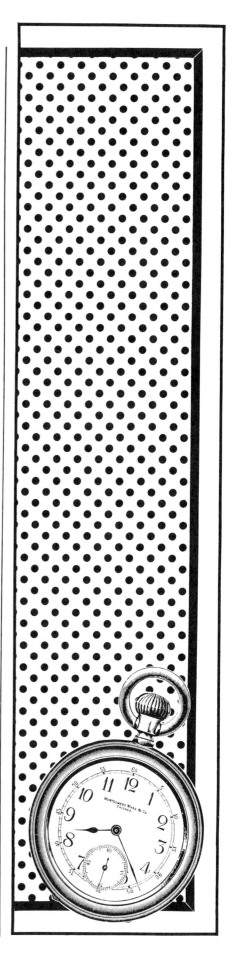

MOVING

Moving is the great American tradition. More people move yearly in the U.S. than the total population of Ghana, Guatemala, Mongolia, and Tunisia. From dorm to apartment to condo we go.

It is a rite of passage. It often means a change in identities, a change in roles, and always a change in the furniture.

Each move is steeped in the same age-old traditions: getting organized, moving out, moving in, and if it's an under-construction move, it means "topping-out."

As we merrily move along across town or across the country, the family traditions are carefully wrapped in tissue to follow the family wherever they go. Moving boxes are marked "Decorations — Christmas Closet," "Family Recipes — Right Kitchen Shelf," "Wedding Pictures — Master Bedroom," "Graduation Scrapbook — Pink Bedroom." Because moves uproot families, break familiar ties, put distance between close relationships, traditions are more important than ever. Traditions are the family security blanket that provides emotional security and a sense of continuity. They should be lovingly marked "Fragile — Handle With Care."

MOVING OUT

GETTING YOUR HOUSE IN ORDER

Getting your house in order means anything from putting on hip boots and a mask and cleaning out the dark corners of the house to examining kid-packed boxes and saying, "Would you pay to move THAT?" Moves set off insecurities and uncertainties. Getting organized helps to calm the savage spirit and get the show on the road.

SPICE IS NICE

In Barbara Friedrich and Sally Hulstrand's book, *Did Somebody Pack the Baby?*, they offer quick tips on how to make a house smell heavenly when a buyer is on the way. "Sprinkle a little nutmeg on a warm burner, and they'll think you just baked an apple pie. Or simmer some bouillon in a pan on the back burner."

They also include a recipe for Castle Spice, "a concoction reportedly used in medieval days to combat the odors of goats, chickens, and chamber pots in the old chateau."

  4 cinnamon sticks
16 whole cloves
  1 teaspoon pickling sauce
  4 teaspoons ground ginger
  2 quarts water

Combine in a large kettle, bring to a boil, and simmer as long as needed.

One of the authors adds, "I always make this at Christmas time too because it smells so great, but it's confusing for the children. When the aroma of Castle Spice wafts through the house, they don't know whether to start packing or write to Santa."

MOVING GEMS

When Lonnie Young moved to Columbus, Ohio, she tackled the job of moving dishes in a flash by sticking one or two paper plates between each china plate.

She wrapped other breakables in tissue paper, then in newspaper. No washing on the other end.

Veteran movers always recommend repairing and rejuvenating furniture and appliances before you move. The repairing and rejuvenating of the moving family usually takes up the most time after the move.

Label boxes carefully. It's hard to tell the treasures from the trash when those boxes come flying off the van. Somehow they all look alike. In *Did Somebody Pack The Baby?,* the authors suggest color-coding boxes and attaching a corresponding color to the door of the room in which those boxes belong. It makes the move move.

GARAGE SALES

Sales signs can be unintentionally misleading. After reading a sign, one child excitedly asked, "Hey, Mom, can we buy a giant?" When three pairs of stunned eyes in the car turned to him, he said, "Well, the sign said 'Giant Sale.' " From then on, the family jointly contemplated buying "yards" at a "Yard Sale" and one, two, or three families at a "Three Family Sale." But they could never decide if a garage, without a house, was a good buy at a "Garage Sale."

Never mind the sign, Garage Sales offer good buys and good ways of getting rid of items you don't want to move. Frances Kuniansky and Shirley Romm, who manage estate sales, say that well-advertised, well-marked, and well-arranged sales are the most successful. They also add that "garage sales offer more security for the homeowner, but when items are sold in the home they seem to take on more value for the buyer and get a better price for the seller."

After the sale, arrange for Goodwill Industries, the Salvation Army, or a thrift house to cart away leftovers. It is a tax deduction.

MOVING SACK

On the morning of the move, one single father gave each child a giant garbage sack. Into each sack went a complete change of clothes, pj's, toothbrush and toothpaste, washcloth and soap, and the bed covers from their beds stripped and rolled up. The sack is the last thing in the car or the van. No matter what the day brings, at least that night the kids will have a place to sleep and can go to bed clean — whether they want to or not.

ONE MAN'S TREASURE

When Penny Yeargen, co-author of the *Atlanta House Book,* moved from California to Atlanta, she had a Neighborhood Going Away Party on moving day morning. "I gave away frozen foods, the entire contents of my refrigerator, plants, and even pets." Then she added, "I didn't really have as much luck with the pets as I did with the frozen pizza."

GOING AWAY GIFTS

"Parting is such sweet sorrow" that we must have a party tomorrow. Moving away parties are a national tradition. Gifts and Going Away Parties are a way of offering emotional support and saying, "Hey, remember me." Put a bow on some of these ideas.

★ A collection of menus from favorite local restaurants or their aprons, bibs, and caps.

★ T-shirts from the hometown sports team, schools and colleges, special events, amusement centers, or street festivals, or a "Pat Your Pet" shirt from the Humane Society.

★ Ingredients for a favorite local recipe that may not be available when friends move from Alabama to Akron.

★ A painting, sketch, watercolor, or pen and ink drawing of the old home in a frame that says, "Home Sweet Home."

★ A new tag for moving pets stamped with their new address. Families can't cope with moving and missing a pet at the same time.

★ "Getting to know you" — A gift subscription to the newspaper or city magazine in the new city.

★ A "Remember Me, I'm The One Who Loves You" gift subscription to the weekend newspaper or city magazine from the old city.

★ A membership to the art association, historical society, or library association in the new city.

★ Polaroid pictures of each guest, couple, or friend with his/her address and birthday on the back of the picture.

★ A new cover for the old phone book — Yellow Pages, too. The need for old numbers always comes up when you need a referral, a reference, or a prescription refilled.

PARTING SHOTS

When George, Marleen, Mandy, and Jeff Pushkar left Larchmont, New York, they packed a lucite frame filled with treasured pictures their neighbors and kids had put together. There were shots of kids in a pyramid, a street banner for Wakeman Place, sledding scenes, and a great composite of neighborhood dogs.

The kids in their neighborhood decorated their car with streamers, tin cans, and a "Just Moving" sign. "As we rolled out of the driveway, they bombed us with confetti," reminisced Marleen.

The inside of the car was filled with notes hidden in secret places. In the glove compartment, the ashtray, under the seat and behind the mirror were notes that read, "We always had so much fun at your house" or "I loved the ...."

BLESS THIS HOUSE

A mezuzah is a ceremonial Hebrew scroll traditionally placed in the doorway of a Jewish house to ask for God's blessing. When Abraham Ribicoff was governor of Connecticut, he had one placed on his doorway. When John N. Dempsey became governor, he left the little prayer in place, sensing a continuing need for God's blessings.

MOVING IN

Home is where the family is. Relocation rituals help those on the move to celebrate a new beginning, a new home. These rituals can be anything that is special and ceremonial: a groom carrying his new bride over the threshold, a certain chair that is always carried into the new house first, or maybe a traditional packing-case picnic at the end of a weary day.

GREAT BEGINNINGS

There is an old Jewish tradition of giving bread, salt, and candles as a moving-in gift. It represents wishes for plenty of food and joy, symbolized by light.

When editor Larry Ashmead moved into his New York apartment, this gift was left at his door. Unaware of the tradition, he thought he had received a stash of cocaine.

A FRESH START

One gift for a new neighbor was a gift for the old neighbor as well. "I always keep a list of phone numbers for the neighbors, the local drugstore, grocery and hardware store, T.V. appliance repairmen, plumbers, fast-food and local restaurants, and police, fire, and emergency numbers on the inside of my kitchen cabinet nearest the phone. Whenever a new neighbor moves in, I xerox the list and give it to them for their kitchen cabinets. When my list gets to be too much of a mess with additions and subtractions, I retype it and we *both* get a neat, fresh start," reported the old neighbor.

DAYS OF OUR LIVES

When Mickey and Maggie Horton on the soap opera *Days of Our Lives* moved into their new house, Dr. and Mrs. Horton took them the family's traditional moving-in gift, a garden basket filled with tools, seeds, and other garden goodies. (Traditions are alive and well — even on the Soaps!)

TAKING ROOT

On moving-in day, in Champaign, Illinois, Adlon Jorgensen sent her new neighbor a beautiful pot of flowers to celebrate the event. Her neighbor later told her, "They sat on a packing case and the fresh bright colors were a charming oasis in the midst of chaos. After the move we took the flowers outside and planted them. We took root together."

HAVE A HANGING

Have a picnic party for all the people "your family and friends have told you to look up." Do it as soon as you arrive so you won't have to make excuses for the house. Call it a "Hanging" and let everyone help you get those pictures up off the floor.

MOVING IN AND EATING OUT

Another neighbor collects menus from neighborhood restaurants or take-out pizza parlors and gives them as a gift to his new neighbors. "The thing I make best for dinner," he added, "is reservations."

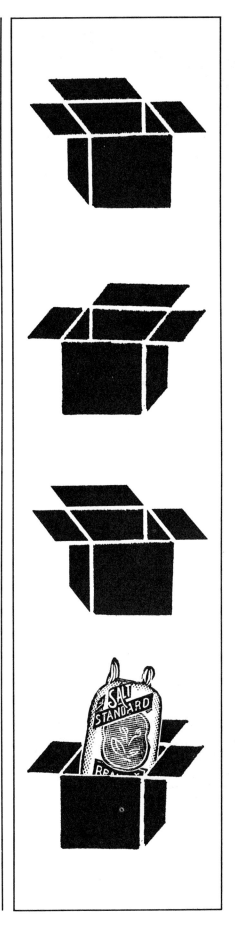

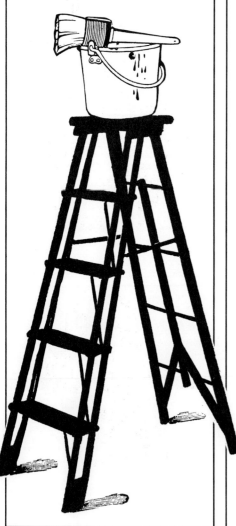

FEELING CONNECTED

There is no greater moving-in tradition than that of using family furniture in the first home. In goes the sofa from Dad's den, Grandmother's chest, the bride's bedroom furniture, the desk from "his" apartment, or Mom's dining room chairs.

Old family furniture can be an unholy collection of styles, eras, and periods. These classics range from Early Attic to Late Salvation Army with a few pieces that missed a period.

Hand-me-downs abound. Passing along family keepsakes offers familiarity, security, comfort and memories. As designer Perry Ellis said about his cherished family pieces, "My house reflects the things I grew up with."

PAINTING PARTIES

The quickest way to get a new look in an old place is with paint. Have a "Beer, Brush and Blue Jean party." Offer cold beer, good sandwiches, and hot brushes.

The host/hostess does the preliminary work: unscrew light switch plates, take down blinds, fill and sand cracks, get out the drop cloths, set up the ladders, dust the corners, and let the rollers roll.

Caterer Gail Prescott of Celebrations created a fortieth birthday party for a man that was a variation of this theme.

The birthday husband and wife had just moved into a large home and had very little furniture. So she designed a redecorating "do."

Brightly colored wallpaper samples were sent out inviting couples to a seated buffet. Drop cloths were used to decorate the tables and paint buckets held the flowers. Boards between ladders were set up everywhere as bars and buffet tables. The house was full of the spirit of redecorating and rejoicing.

GETTING KNOWN
IN THE NEIGHBORHOOD

Bob Douglas moved from Philadelphia before the rest of his family. When wife Dianne and their children arrived two months later, he greeted them at the airport with a limousine. They were driven through their new neighborhood and when they arrived at their front door he had also arranged to have one hundred balloons welcome them. Now, that's the way to get known in the neighborhood!

MOVING PICTURE STORIES

Families whose businesses constantly keep them on the move can begin a picture history of "The Paynes — Places We Have Lived." Each picture comes fully developed with its own particular set of memories. These are fun to pull out and reminisce about on snowy winter nights.

OPEN DOOR POLICY

One Florida family left the security of a small town for the Big Apple. They had formal cards engraved with their new address, officially declaring it the Marianna, Florida, Embassy in New York City. The welcome mat for old neighbors was out.

HOW TO FAKE IT AS A NATIVE

Get into the spirit of the new city. Treat your new city as if it's the place you will spend the rest of your life. Take a city tour and take pictures of family members on the "tallest building," the "oldest landmark," or "the newest sports center" to send to friends you've left behind.

Learn the language. Minnesotanians do not say "hello" the same way they do in Mississippi. They don't say a lot of things the same. You often need a translator, but the quicker you learn the language the more like a native you'll feel.

Join a group in the new city. Ideas that are "stolen thunder" from the old town will be "news flashes" in the new one.

Naturalize the family with hometown traditional foods. Cook local recipes from local cookbooks and ask for help from natives. Sourdough bread is the pride of San Francisco that the crowd from Kansas may have never even tasted.

NEW HOME TRADITIONS

Not all families have the good fortune to build a house, so the traditions surrounding those under-construction moves are usually borrowed, stolen, or made up. Share and enjoy.

A STUD PARTY

When the Chamberses' new home was under construction, they kept a collection of colorful magic markers by the framed-in front door. They invited family, friends, neighbors, and workers to autograph a stud while the house was taking shape, thereby making them an original part of the house forever.

There were fifty original signers of the Declaration of Independence. There is no telling how many original signers there were of this landmark.

GRAUMAN'S CHINESE DRIVEWAY

There is no greater American tradition than handprints in wet cement. Whenever fresh cement is poured on your new construction site, be sure that the family celebrities make their mark for posterity. Date this historical deed.

TOPPING OUT PARTY

It is a Scandinavian custom to tie the branch of a living tree to the topmost part of a house once the roof has been framed. It symbolizes good luck.

Celebrate a "topping out" with a construction site picnic. Invite the architect, contractor, and all the workers. Serve sandwiches, Po' Boys (which will probably be appropriate by this time), and cold drinks.

THE UP-SHOT OF IT ALL

A stage-by-stage picture album of a couple's first custom-built home was a unique moving-in gift. The photographer came by every few days to record the highlights from groundbreaking through decorating. The house and the album were picture-perfect.

FUNERALS

Funerals celebrate the life of a loved one. It is a time for a family reunion and for remembering funny stories, shared experiences, the good times and the bad, the joys and the heartbreaks. It is also a time when the family becomes acquainted with new members — babies, brides, grooms, step-relations, and friends. It is the extended family sharing a loss. The ritual of family and friends gathering provides an emotional support system, a tug on the family security blanket once again.

FUNERALS

CHANGING TIMES

In the early years of America, families lived close together, and death and dying were part of the natural process of life. Most people died at home, and even as late as the 1960s, in many rural areas, the body was viewed in the family parlor.

Today, many people die in hospitals with family members scattered across the country. Young people are removed from death and the aging process as a personal experience.

The awareness of death comes to them primarily through television. Cop shows, westerns, and the 6 o'clock news bring death into the home, often without the sense of continuity and love that family closeness can provide.

GETTING INVOLVED

Changing attitudes of society have affected the traditions of this special time. Pallbearers, once an all-male coterie, now share the honor with females. Women have served in this capacity in both military and civilian services.

Mrs. Kennedy's quiet dignity and stoic behavior during her husband's funeral had a marked effect on the public demeanor of other grieving families.

The Kennedy family's participation in the eulogy of John F. Kennedy encouraged more and more family members and friends to take part in this ritual.

Funeral services vary. Some are very personal; others are more formal. In life, Bob Savitt had a tradition of holding hands and saying a prayer at the table whenever the family was together. At the close of his funeral service, the congregation held hands and said a quiet prayer. It was a sharing, a moving moment.

Other services reflect a more impersonal attitude. At Margaret Scholz's funeral, her favorite clergyman mentioned her name only once. It was an Episcopal service, and it is her denomination's belief that all people are equal in God's sight; therefore, all members, involved or inactive, rich or poor, male or female, are buried in the same way. However, her oldest grandson Rufus did serve as an acolyte, which added great warmth to his beloved ''Nane's'' service.

CHANGING RHYTHMS (MUSIC)

Music reflects many different changes in life. In the early times music for funerals was traditional, more closely associated with the church. Today, it has a more contemporary sound.

Great funeral marches composed by Beethoven, Handel, and Chopin; slow, mournful anthems; and congregational hymn-singing are the traditional sounds of funeral music.

''Today,'' as one funeral director said, ''there is less slow-walking and sad-singing.'' Many times a folk service is held for a young person. The music is contemporary and a guitar, rather than organ, accompanies the songs. One young pallbearer commented, ''There isn't any difference in the kind of respect that is shown. This kind of service is very meaningful and very relevant for young people."

$$$ AND TRADITIONS

Economics play a key role in changing traditions. Black, the traditional color of mourning, was an expensive custom, because a black suit or dress was often worn only for funerals. Arm bands allowed people to show their respect in everyday clothes. Today, however, mourning bands are rarely seen, and the tradition of wearing black is declining.

Other cost-cutting measures have affected the tradition of death and dying. The custom of bell-ringing to announce a death was well established when John Donne wrote the line "... for whom the bell tolls." As the cost of the bell-ringers became more expensive, the bells no longer tolled.

Sunday was a traditional day for funerals. Today, because of overtime costs, burials are rarely held on this day.

Rising costs have also increased the number of cremations. Immediate-disposition companies will pick up the body, deliver it directly to a crematorium, and dispose of the ashes if requested. Expenses for a casket and other funeral services are therefore avoided. Memorial services may also be held with family and friends. St. Anne's Church in Atlanta, as well as many other churches, has established a memorial garden for the ashes. Burials in the church cemetery go back to the age-old tradition of being buried on holy ground.

BEING THERE

Attendance at funerals is yet another cause for a change in tradition. An hourly worker can have his pay docked when he attends the funeral of someone other than his blood relative. "This is bound to affect people when their neighbors, co-workers, and friends die," a funeral director noted.

Mary P. Schneck's solution to this problem may have created a new tradition. "After my husband had his first heart attack, he asked me to plan an evening funeral for him in the event he did not recover. He could not see why anyone should take time off from work to attend a funeral when it could be held in the evening.

"When he had the second attack, which was fatal, I planned an evening funeral for friends and family and a private burial the next day just for family members. It was a very personal experience for our family, which we now cherish."

DO-IT-YOURSELF FUNERAL
PLANNING AHEAD

Today many people are making pre-arrangements for their own service. President Franklin Roosevelt may have established this pattern as early as 1937. Although he shunned the subject of death, he did write explicit directions for his own funeral. He spelled out how long the service should be, who should attend, and what his marker should look like.

Today, pre-arrangements are made for many reasons. People with small families or no survivors or those with children scattered across the

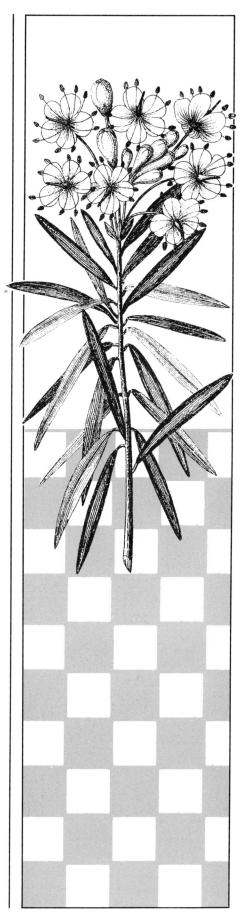

country find it comforting to know that all of their affairs are in order. Terminally ill patients and couples who have just been through this experience also make their own arrangements to spare their survivors.

Others prearrange their services because of financial considerations. They want to set up their own financial guidelines.

It's Your Choice, the Practical Guide to Planning Funerals is a publication of the American Association of Retired Persons. It is available by writing to It's Your Choice, 400 South Edward Street, Mt. Prospect, Illinois 60056, and enclosing a check or money order for $4.95.

Pre-arrangements, for whatever reason, give survivors the personal satisfaction of knowing that they have carried out the wishes of their loved ones.

After one older couple, Peg and Hub Scholz, completed their arrangements, they said, "We went out and celebrated, celebrated that we had done it and celebrated that we were still here to enjoy our martinis."

A LAST GREAT CELEBRATION

A wise mother once said that when anyone in the family went on a trip, the ones who stayed at home always "missed" the most. This is true for funerals.

Funerals are special goodbyes. They are meant to celebrate the life of a loved one, to pay him special tribute, and to give comfort and solace to those who will be here to do the "missing."

There is a saying that "a funeral is a person's last great party and he misses it only by a few days." Gather the family close together for support and for the celebration of this last great party.

The funeral for Rosalie Hanes Rice was a "Celebration of Life," said retailer Larry Lewis. Mrs. Rice, daughter of P.H. Hanes of Hanes Hosiery, was buried in a Moravian service in Winston-Salem, North Carolina. "The church was radiant with spring flowers in every color of the spectrum. Pink roses, baby's breath, and daisies covered her casket. The service highlighted her life, her family, and her contributions to the community. At the graveside, a six-piece brass ensemble with French horns and a tuba accompanied the singing of family and friends and, as is the Moravian custom, 'piped her into Heaven.' "

CELEBRATIONS OF LIFE

DONORS-MEMORIALS-DONATIONS

Through death, new life often begins for others. Death has often given people motivation, an urgent need to accomplish something so that tragedy can have meaning. Dreams don't end, but are kept alive through others.

Milton Bevington, who lost his wife in the Orly plane crash, set up the Children's Foundation for emotionally disturbed children in her memory. He realized that when relatives and friends asked, "What can we do?," together they could do a lot of good if their efforts went in one direction.

The following thoughts on personal donations (organs), charitable

84

donations, and memorials speak meaningfully to the fact that those who are dead still contribute to the life cycle of others.

ORGAN DONORS AND TRANSPLANTS

Medical research and technology have made possible the "gift of life." Through the donations of eyes, lungs, heart, liver, pancreas, and other vital tissues and organs at the time of death, new life for others becomes possible.

When Eve was created from the rib of Adam, it made her, as one cartoon caption said, "not only the first woman but the first transplant." History has not handled the subject of transplants as gently. Transplanting of vital organs was thought ghoulish, pagan, and evil. The continued success of medical science has enabled the Age of Transplantation to come into being.

By 1971, all states had adopted the Uniform Anatomical Gift Act. It provides that "anyone of sound mind or body, eighteen years or older, may donate all or part of his body for medical purposes after death." A donor's card can save precious minutes which are often critical to the success of the transplant. Uniform Organ Donor Cards and information are available through foundations such as the Lions Eye Bank or through all state driver's license bureaus.

DONATIONS

There is a Greek saying that "as long as someone speaks your name, you will continue to live." What more meaningful way to keep the spirit of a loved one or friend alive than by making a donation in his memory. Donations and memorials have contributed to research for cancer, aid for crippled children, tapes for the blind, and meals for senior citizens. They have made possible new ministries for churches and synagogues, new equipment for hospitals, new programs for the arts, new courses for schools. Today, more than $10 billion is given annually in charitable contributions for human welfare.

MEMORIALS

Memorials are gifts given by a family in celebration of the life of a family member. One of the most substantial memorials in the country was set up in 1948 in memory of Joseph N. Pew, founder of Sun Oil, by his wife. Their four children administer the funds from this memorial trust to address a broad range of human needs.

The John F. Kennedy Center for Performing Arts in Washington, D.C., is a national memorial to the late president.

Parents have established family memorials which range from a small school garden to the support of an annual church camper.

In 1962, following a tour of Europe, 122 of Atlanta's leading citizens were killed in a plane crash in Orly, France. Plans were developed to construct a cultural arts center in their memory. "We will not let this tragedy be just a tragedy. We will use it as an inspiration. Through what we do, the people who died will live from generation to generation," said James Carmichael, one of the primary forces behind the center.

In 1968, the Atlanta Memorial Arts Center was opened. Through the death of these citizens, new life for the arts was born.

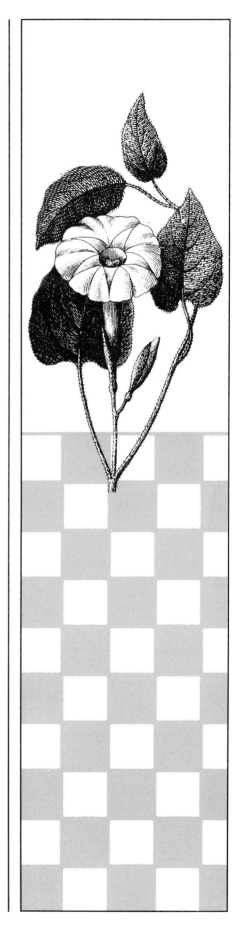

LIFE APPRECIATION TRIBUTES

Tributes are expressions of love and appreciation for the life of a loved one. They come in many forms. The following celebrations of life are to be shared.

A SPECIAL PRAYER

When sixteen-year-old Greg Mohr was killed in a car accident, his family wanted other people to note how fragile life is. Their acknowledgement card best expressed their love and their loss:

> Our prayer for you
> is that you glimpse through him,
> and through his death,
> how rich and sweet and fragile life is;
> and how much it is to be cherished.
> Our Thanks
> The family of Greg Mohr

TWENTY-FOUR SPRINGS

Twenty-four-year-old Martin Westmoreland was a young architect just beginning his career in San Francisco. He was murdered one night after working late.

"While the investigation was going on, his mother wrote a tribute to her son. I insisted that it be read at the funeral and from that point on she began to compile a booklet of Martin's life and death as an expression of her love," said Martin's father.

The result was a lovely booklet, entitled *Twenty-Four Springs*. It was a brief chronicle of Martin's life, newspaper accounts of the tragedy

Our prayer for you

is that you glimpse through him,

and through his death,

how rich and sweet and fragile life is;

and how much it is to be cherished

Our Thanks

The family of Greg Mohr

and of the funeral service, other tributes, and excerpts from Martin's letters from college and travels.

WORDS OF LOVE

In 1982, Phil Heiner, husband, father, and a talented lawyer, found out he had cancer. He lived only three more months, but during this time he kept a diary and wrote letters to his family. Part of his letters were read at his funeral service and serve as an inspiration for all those who share his love of life:

When you see the success in the mirror
    and you're impressed with the image . . .
Ask how you put it all together
    and whom you lost by the wayside . . .
Success is relative; Love and Friends
    are absolute.

WHEN A PARENT DIES

In Jill Krementz's book, *How It Feels When a Parent Dies*, young people talk about their personal losses. It is a meaningful book for young people and includes these two farewell tributes.

Gail Gugle, age 7, at her father's service:

We put seven red roses on top of the coffin, one for each member of the family. Red is supposed to be the color of love, and the rose is supposed to be the flower of love.

John During, age 15:

The night before the funeral, I drew a picture for her [his mother] and wrote a note on it, asking her to wait in heaven for all of us. I gave it to Daddy to put in the coffin with her, and even though she was dead, I like to think she got that last message from me.

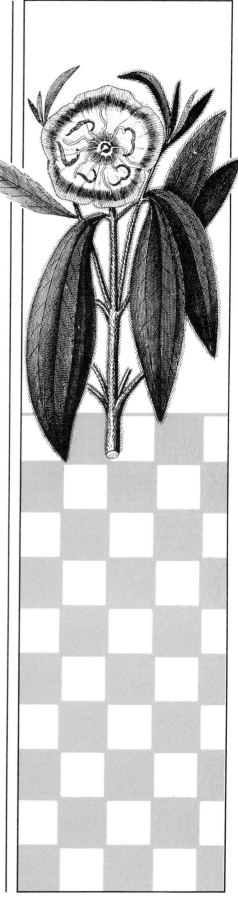

"Within this universe of friends there exists a special form of friendship, which goes to the essence of life itself."

S. Phillip Heiner
March, 1982

The family of
Phil Heiner
deeply appreciates
your kind expression of friendship

MAKE THIS A HAPPY FAMILY REUNION

An Alabama father set the tone for his final celebration in a note he wrote in his last week of life:

> I want no weeping and wailing over me. I will already have left for a better world. Make this a happy family reunion like we had after Mother's funeral. I have lived a happy and complete life. What more can a person ask?

NO PERSON WITH A FAMILY EVER DIED

The loving continuity of life is best described in *Dandelion Wine*, Ray Bradbury's story about the impending death of a beloved grandmother. One young grandson comes to her bed and tearfully seeks comfort for the loss he is beginning to feel. He says to her, "But, Grandma, you won't be here tomorrow." She turned a small hand mirror from herself to the boy. He looked at her face and himself in the mirror and then at her face again as she said, "Tomorrow morning I'll get up at seven and wash behind my ears; I'll run to church with Charlie Woodman; I'll picnic at Electric Park; I'll swim, run barefoot, fall out of trees, chew spearmint gum. ..." Then later on she said it best, "No person with a family ever died."

MOST APPRECIATED KINDNESS

Many people who have known the loss of a loved one talk about the kindness friends and family offered. The following is their list:

★ People coming by the house to express their care, concern, and sympathy. People who took time to come to the service. "I needed to know that people cared, that they shared my grief, that I wasn't alone. Anyone who feels hesitant about visiting should realize they are not imposing, they are supporting," said one widow.

★ A friend or relative can organize shifts to answer the door or take calls. In most instances this person sets the tone for the caller. He lets them know how the family is coping and gives information about the service. He/she is there to thank callers for their visit, if the family is not seeing visitors, and to ask them to sign the visitors' book. It is a courtesy when signing the book to put your name, address AND zip code. Others will follow and save the family the task of having to look them up when they send acknowledgement cards.

★ Take a card file to keep up with the names of people who bring food or do other kindnesses. Thoughtful notations on cards make it easier for the family to acknowledge kindness later.

★ Organize meals. In Quincy, Florida, several people bring the same main dishes for the family and friends after the service. It coordinates the menu and provides a lovely meal.

★ Offer to pick up relatives and friends at the airport.

★ Offer to let them stay in your home.

★ Offer to make local or long distance calls, especially if you have access to a WATS line. Remember to tell friends and acquaintances about the death later if they are out of town at the time.

★ Offer to keep the family's children. Be sure to ask the family how they want the subject of death handled.

★ Take care of routine household chores: getting groceries, picking up laundry, pressing clothes, arranging flowers, washing dishes, or making beds. Any kindness that is done — from sweeping the walk to painting a room — so that the deceased will be well remembered is thoughtful.

★ Offer to go to the funeral home to help make final arrangements. You can provide emotional security and objectiveness, if needed.

★ Pack a small basket of food for the family to take if the burial service is out of town.

★ Send notes to the family of the deceased. Most people commented that "a two-sentence note" meant more than a card, but all expressions were appreciated. Notes remembering personal experiences are special.

★ Make a personal call if you have shared a similar loss, the loss of a child, a spouse, or a parent. Personal experiences provide insight and comfort to those who are in need of support.

★ Arrange to help with acknowledgement cards. Looking up addresses and zip codes is taxing. Friends who come by for an hour or two are of great assistance and consolation.

★ Teenagers can be a great comfort to each other when there is a loss. "When my brother died, friends came by and just sat with me. We didn't talk, they were just there. It was important to me to know that it was important to them."

A mother of three who lost her son said, "Seeing my children being comforted by their friends helped me. I knew they were getting love and support. Teenagers share a great openness and friendship toward each other. This closeness is important in bad times, as well as the good.

★ Books are lovely gifts. This is the Information Age, and there are many noteworthy books on death and dying that can give solace, day or night.

One mother who had lost a child commented, "There are suddenly so many changes between you and your husband, in your sex life, with money, travel, or in daily life. Just reading that these were common problems was a great comfort and relief."

Book suggestions:
Getting Through the Night: Finding Your Way After the Loss of a Loved One — Eugenia Price
The Bereaved Parent — Harriett Sarnoff Schiff
How It Feels When a Parent Dies — Jill Krementz
When Bad Things Happen to Good People — Harold S. Kushner
A Grief Observed — C.S. Lewis

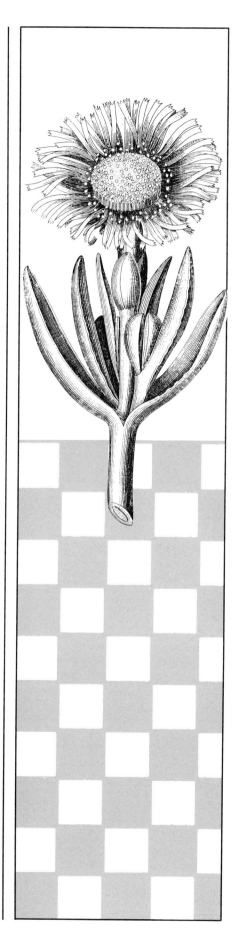

CALENDAR DAYS

Holidays add excitement and anticipation to the calendar. They stop work, break the routine, and add ritual and romance.

Secular as well as religious holidays have their roots in the ritual of worship. Most holidays began as pagan celebrations of nature: man's celebration of the spring planting or the fall harvest, his thanksgiving for the sun or the rain. Church festivals took the place of many pagan customs and gave them new meaning.

Today, as in ancient times, holidays add life. Christmas and Hanukkah, Easter, and Passover celebrate and enhance our religious life. Thanksgiving and the Fourth of July give us the flavor of home-grown, made-in-America celebrations. Halloween, Valentine's, and New Year's combine old pagan customs with Christian feast days to give us mystery, romance, and a sense of new beginnings. Mother's Day and Father's Day remind us of our roots. Celebrate the holidays. They are genuine, certified, card-carrying tradition days.

THE NEW YEAR

Revelers around the world celebrate the traditions of the New Year at different times of the years. Egyptians got into the spirit of the New Year in June, not January. The Chinese celebrate between January and February, and the holy ritual of the Jewish New Year falls in late September. If you need a fresh start or a reason to celebrate, mark your calendar and start your own New Year today.

In ancient Rome, the first day of the year honored Janus, the god of gates and doors, endings and beginnings. He had two faces and looked forward and backwards. The Romans may have set the tone for the old and the new year, but revelers in every country have added their festive customs to this celebration. The English and the Swiss made merry with masks and costumes. The Chinese celebrated with fireworks. The Austrians and Germans tooted in the New Year with trumpet fanfare, and the Dutch invited everybody over for an open house. The Scots rang out the old year with strains of Robert Burns's "Auld Lang Syne." To date, no country has yet to lay claim to the traditional hangover.

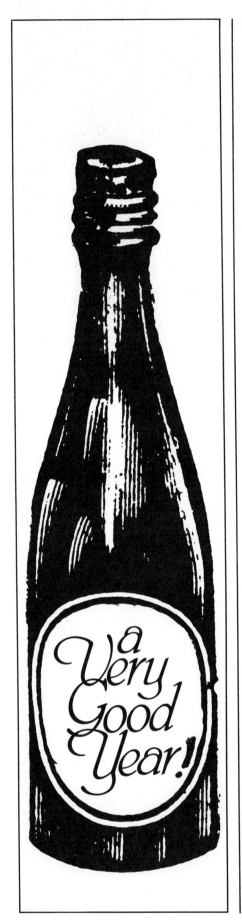

NEW YEAR'S EVE

The celebration of New Year's Eve is met with mixed reaction. Some love the fierce merrymaking; others loathe the forced gaiety and relentless good cheer; but all seem to celebrate in some fashion. One couple marks the date with a small, black-tie dinner party. Two other couples welcome in the New Year together at a posh restaurant. Three families annually pop the cork at a New Year's evening of entertainment created and produced by their children. Still others escape the call to congregate by leaving town. Whatever your pleasure on this oldest of eves, there are plenty of traditions to borrow or burgle.

PRE-NEW YEAR'S COCKTAILS

The invitation reads, "Cocktails, New Years Eve, 7-9." Early merrymakers stop by on their way to late evening festivities. It is a jubilant gathering of many ages and groups. From 10 o'clock on, the host and hostess have a very private party.

A CELEBRATION SUCCESS

South Carolinian John Reichard has three secrets for a successful, large, annual New Year's Eve party: Invite three different crowds of people so guests will know some people and meet others. Use a small house so people are really "together," and order seven hundred pounds of ice! The party was abandoned after seven years due to its popularity and overcrowding. "It's a tribute to its success that people showed up for this celebration three years *after* it had been abandoned."

COSTUMED REVELERS

A bachelors' club known as the Nine O'Clocks has an annual imaginative costume ball on New Year's Eve. This gala is tailored to an annual theme. There are prizes for individual, couple, and group costumes. Brainstorming for crazy and creative costume ideas is part of the fun of this major social event.

JANUARY

S	M	T	W	TH	F	S
1	2	3	4	5	6	7
8	9	10	11	12	13	14
15	16	17	18	19	20	21
22	23	24	25	26	27	28
29	30	31				

FEBRUARY

				1	2	3	4
5	6	7	8	9	10	11
12	13	14	15	16	17	18
19	20	21	22	23	24	25
26	27	28				

MARCH

				1	2	3	4
5	6	7	8	9	10	11
12	13	14	15	16	17	18
19	20	21	22	23	24	25
26	27	28	29	30	31	

APRIL

						1
2	3	4	5	6	7	8
9	10	11	12	13	14	15
16	17	18	19	20	21	22
23	24	25	26	27	28	29
30						

MAY

	1	2	3	4	5	6
7	8	9	10	11	12	13

NEW YEAR'S DAY

MARK THE DATE

Every country in the world, and all American football fans, celebrate New Year's Day. The annual New Year's Day celebration of the Tournament of Roses kicks off the year. Stan and Sally Wild grew up in Pasadena, California, and as teens always worked on the floats for the parade. Now married and living in Michigan, Sally starts the day just like the Romans by giving Stan a gift. She gives him a rose "as a memory of our first meeting."

KING FOR A DAY

Carl Dendee has his birthday on New Year's Day. He eats his favorite food, watches his favorite football games, and always plays golf on his day, rain, sun, or snow. He is just superstitious enough to "know" that what you do on New Year's Day, you will do all year round.

A BITE OF GOOD LUCK

It is a foolhardy southerner who does not have the traditional hog jowls and black-eyed peas on New Year's Day to insure luck and money for the year. "Cabbage, or any food that swells when it's cooked, is an alternative to black-eyes," says an expert. However, not many southerners would risk a substitute.

SOUPER BOWL

There's the Rose Bowl and the Sugar Bowl and the Orange Bowl, but the Joe Ashers have the Souper Bowl, an annual New Year's open

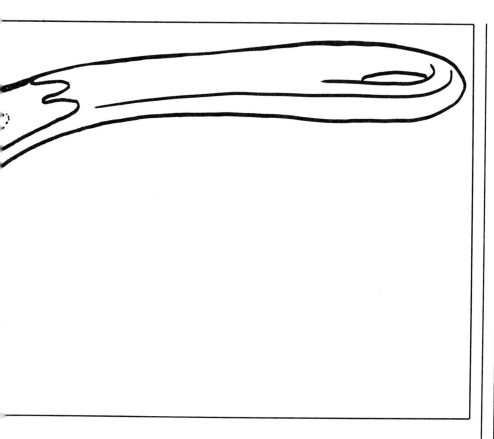

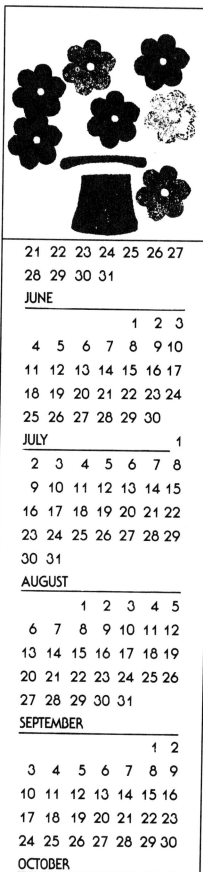

house with friends, family, football, and food. The menu includes hog jowls and black-eyed peas and homemade vegetable soup.

A BRAND NEW DAY

Unwrapping the New Year Calendar is a tradition in one family. They open it and ceremoniously mark the special events of the year in red crayon. They mark birthdays, vacations, and holidays. It gives everyone a handle on time and events to look forward to together.

NEW YEAR'S DAY BY THE BOOK

When Boyce Lokey Martin and her brothers and sisters were children, they each received special books on New Year's Day from their mother. Each child was given a beautifully illustrated edition appropriate for his age. It was a wonderful, looked-forward-to gift that would have been overlooked on Christmas Day. "We continued this tradition and share libraries and our pride of collecting with our children. Now as grandparents, we begin a third generation of New Year's books."

The influence of books must have been particularly strong for Boyce Lokey. She grew up and married writer Harold Martin.

BETTER THAN A RESOLUTION

This family ritual, reported in *McCall's,* started with an inventory for a fire insurance policy. After the job was done, the wife said, "Now we have a list of the things we have, but what about the intangibles?" The couple then made a list of intangibles — a happiness inventory — love, trust, health, sense of humor, etc. They review it yearly and make additions.

21	22	23	24	25	26	27
28	29	30	31			

JUNE

				1	2	3
4	5	6	7	8	9	10
11	12	13	14	15	16	17
18	19	20	21	22	23	24
25	26	27	28	29	30	

JULY

						1
2	3	4	5	6	7	8
9	10	11	12	13	14	15
16	17	18	19	20	21	22
23	24	25	26	27	28	29
30	31					

AUGUST

		1	2	3	4	5
6	7	8	9	10	11	12
13	14	15	16	17	18	19
20	21	22	23	24	25	26
27	28	29	30	31		

SEPTEMBER

					1	2
3	4	5	6	7	8	9
10	11	12	13	14	15	16
17	18	19	20	21	22	23
24	25	26	27	28	29	30

OCTOBER

1	2	3	4	5	6	7

VALENTINES

Valentine's Day celebrates the tradition of love. You can say it and you can show it in many ways, but each expression sends out the simple message, "I care."

A FEBRUARY OF LOVE OR 29 INSTANT IDEAS FOR VALENTINE'S DAY

(or any day for lovables, live-ins, and lovers)

★ On Valentine's morning, Barbara Feingold stuck a 3 x 5 card for her husband on the shower head that said, "Who loves ya', baby?" The next day, he put it in her lipstick drawer. They have been passing it around from secret place to secret place ever since and not a word has ever been spoken.

★ Make valentine-shaped cinnamon toast for breakfast: butter toast, sprinkle with cinnamon sugar, cut with heart shape cookie cutter.

★ Embroider I LOVE YOU on a pillow case. It takes twenty-three big stitches.

★ Do something "they" have been begging you to do: mend it, lend it, hook it, cook it, or find it. This is a no-cost love effort.

★ Enclose a valentine in the lunch box, briefcase, or pocketbook for a surprise smile during the day.

★ Valentine codes are an old English Valentine tradition. Hang notes all over the house that are written or signed in codes. A-26, B-25, C-24. You may gain a little "cupid quiet" while they decipher the message.

★ Lock up your love. Give someone a gift of a combination lock. The unlatch code: 9--12, 21, 22--21 (figure this out yourself).

★ Make someone's favorite meal or everyone's favorite dish. It doesn't matter if it's weird, everyone will like something. Or make a Valentine cake. This English tradition requires putting a love charm

(dime store favors) in the batter. Put in several so everyone gets a lucky slice. (Eat with care. An English ambassador got more than he expected from his Valentine cake — a broken tooth!)

★ Decorate with posters that say "Make Love, Not War," "Love Thy Neighbor and Thy Sister," "To Be Loved, Be Lovable." Leave them up all year.

★ Remember your own parents — send them some red hots or candy. They want to be loved, too.

★ Put a fresh spring bouquet in the house to celebrate this original 2000-year-old Roman mating rite, Lupercalia. Saint Valentine joined in the celebration later.

★ Put a red ribbon on the family pet — animal, that is. When you pat the puppy, you're telling him with your touch that you care. Do the same for your other pets. Keep in touch.

★ Go the post office and buy a sheet of Robert Indiana's "Love" stamps. Use them all year and spread the word.

★ Rub noses. That is the way Eskimos kiss.

★ Give a gift from the heart. If you are over seventeen, give blood to the American Red Cross or make a donation to the Heart Fund in honor of those you love.

★ Carry a pocketful of chocolate kisses with you and inquire, "Wanna kiss?" One dumbstruck teenage Romeo walking in the school corridor replied to his Juliet, "Right here?"

★ Give a valentine to the postman. Except for Christmas, this is the heaviest day of mail all year.

★ Love in bloom. Give a single flower. This is appreciated by male or female. Teenagers at The Westminster Schools sell and deliver single flowers each Valentine's Day to raise money for charity. For one dollar, they will deliver a white carnation as a symbol of friendship or a red one to signify love.

101

St. Valentine's Day - 1976

★ Poetry is the tradition on February 14. "The rose is red, The violet is blue, Lilies are fair and so are you" is a verse that originated in the 1700s. Borrow this one, make up your own, or buy a small book of verse as a friendship gift: Kahlil Gibran's *The Prophet,* Joan Walsh Anglund's *A Friend Is Someone Who Likes You,* Shel Silverstein's *A Light in the Attic,* or Elizabeth Barrett Browning's famous sonnet that begins "How do I love thee?..." are poetic possibilities.

★ Practice and greet special people with:
Je t'aime (French) "Zhe tem"
Ich liebe dich (German) "Eesh lee-bah deesh"
Ti amo (Italian) "Tee ah-mo"
Te amo (Spanish) "Tay ah-mo"
Jag alskar dig (Swedish) "Yag el-skah day"

★ Stick a heart on anything and it becomes a valentine. Example: a family photo, dinner glasses, a jar of sweet pickles, or the bathroom mirror.

★ Seal all valentines with loving messages: S.W.A.K. — sealed with a kiss, A.F.F. — a friend forever, 👁 ❤ 𝒰 — I love you. The return address is Isle of View!

★ Choose a record with "love" or "heart" in the title. Dedicate it on a disc jockey's show. If your love misses it, someone will hear it and pass on the message.

★ Place the postage stamp upside down on a letter. It means I love you.

★ All the world loves a lover. Invite some friends to a party. Have them come as famous lovers. Or, as each guest arrives, pin the name of a lover on his/her back. Each guest must find out his name by "yes" and "no" questions and find his mate, who becomes his dinner partner.

★ Take the hearts out of two decks of cards and use them as placecards.

★ Make your own love stamp to personalize store-bought valentines. Place thumb on stamp pad and make two prints in a V shape. Carve a heart on a rubber eraser and stamp, stamp, stamp.

★ Wear something red. It's a flattering color on everyone.

★ According to Hoyle, "Hearts is an exciting sometimes hilarious game, suitable for young and old and therefore a great family favorite." Start a continuing game of hearts. Play two or three hands each evening. Keep a running score for the month. (Hoyle's simplified *Guide to Popular Card Games* by Walter Gibson, Doubleday & Co.)

★ Valentine's is overloaded with tales and legends of how this love festival began. Take advantage of this oversupply and add to it. Have an "Ancient Customs I Just Made Up" supper. Encourage each of your loving archers to make up his own original version of its origin. Recreate once again the thrilling story of Prince Val and Tiny. Relive the epic saga of how Prince Val wooed and won the hand of Little Tiny and how they yelled as they rode out of sight, "Happy Big V Day to all and to all a Good Heart!"

MOTHER'S DAY

Everybody has a mother. It's a tradition. Mothers are the source of life and whether that life turns out to belong to a corporate chief or petty thief, that mother still deserves recognition. "I remember mama" is the focus of this day.

Anna Jarvis, whose tireless efforts led to the establishment, in 1911, of Mother's Day as a national observance, was in the end in great despair over the commercialization of this day. For this reason, mothers and children seem to agree that in celebrating this holiday, "simple is best." It's the thought that counts.

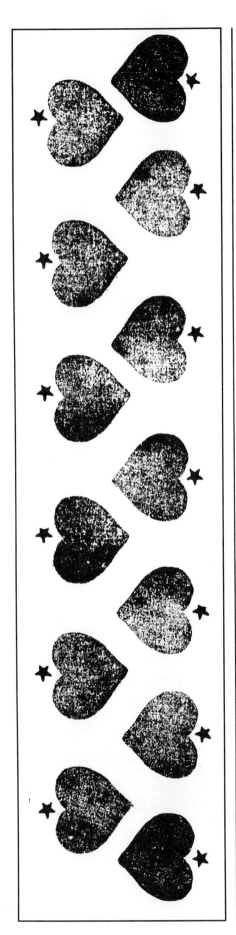

THOUGHTFUL THOUGHTS FOR MOTHER'S DAY REMEMBRANCE

Mother's Day is now big business for florists, candy-makers, Ma Bell, and Western Union. All are fine, as long as they include the personal touch.

★ Mother's Day is the time for a thank-you note, personally written. Here's one that's the greatest: "Dear Momma, it's Mother's day and I'm first in line, To tell the world 'The Greatest' is grateful you're mine! For raising and teaching, the world's prettiest son, Between you and me, you're Number One!"

Mohammed Ali, 1977 (*Ladies' Home Journal*)

★ The daughter of a woman in a nursing home invited two of her mother's friends (also in the home) to lunch. She brought some of her mother's best china for the table and prepared some of her mother's recipes.

★ Mother's Day is the third biggest church-going day. It is traditional that those with a living mother wear a red carnation; those whose mother has died honor her memory with a white one.

★ "I love the mess of my breakfast-in-bed gift and the children's pride in their presentation."

★ "Every year we give Mom our love along with a basket of bright red geraniums for her front step."

★ "For weeks following Mother's Day, my desk is covered with the tearstained letters of mothers who have been forgotten."

Abigail Van Buren (Dear Abby)

FATHER'S DAY

Father's Day is a new tradition. Today not only are babies born, but so are full-fledged daddies. After attending the birth of their baby, these daddies also appear rosy-cheeked and cooing from the delivery room. "It's time fathers were recognized officially," said Senator Margaret Chase Smith, who led the campaign to get Father's Day formally established as a national holiday in 1972. There is a bond between father and child today as never before. As one dad put it, "We've come a long way, baby and me."

Instilling Mother's Day and Father's Day traditions in youngsters is often the role of the "other" parent. Even though the honoree is not *your* parent, children first need to see an example of loving kindness toward parents in order to imitate it.

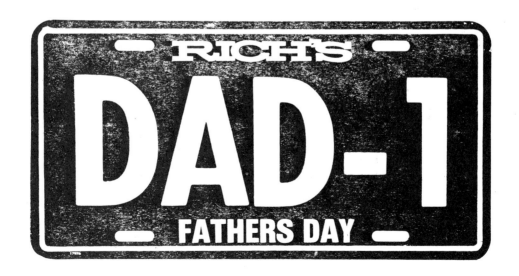

DESIGNER DAD

A crayon drawing of Dad translates into an exclusive, designer T-shirt. Artists should use dark colors and a heavy hand with the crayons on a separate piece of paper. DAD must be written backwards to appear correct on the shirt. Place the crayon drawing on a white T-shirt and iron at "T-shirt temperature." It suits Dad to a T.

Most dads are more into T's than ties. T-shirt shops have transfers on every subject, from Dad's favorite car to his favorite beverage. They even have formal white tie-and-tails T's. Teens especially take to this idea.

I LOVE YOU

Former newspaper editor Jack Spalding's gang of seven is very modest about the cards they make each year. Sometimes they're small and crayoned, sometimes they're in the form of a collaborative family poster. They all say "I love you." With Father's Day and Mother's Day, it is the thought that counts.

JUST DADDY AND ME

The debutante season in Atlanta begins in the summer. A Father and Daughter brunch is a traditional party. Fathers and daughters share introductions, good food, and a fun time with each other. It is their special date on this special day.

108

THE
FOURTH
OF
JULY

INDEPENDENCE DAY

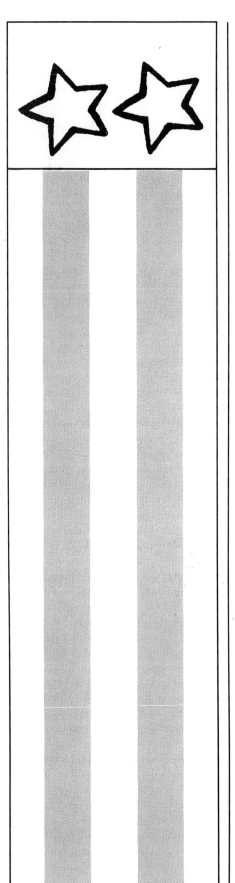

"GOD BLESS AMERICA, LAND THAT I LOVE"

Independence Day, the Fourth of July, offers an opportunity to celebrate and to steep your family in the traditions and ideals that make America great.

America begins at home. Brew up a dose of old-fashioned principles and patriotism and give a child a small dose each day.

Let a child know what you admire, what's important to you. It doesn't take him long to catch on to the fact that you don't like messy rooms, stringy hair, and feet on the sofa. He hears that constantly. He also needs to hear constantly that you hold dear his cheerfulness, particularly in bad times; his courage when it's a quiet thing; the respect he gives to those who earn it; and any, and all, respect that he earns for himself. He needs to hear that you are proud that he doesn't cheat in cards, in class, or on his classmates and that you love his spirit and his fight for independence, even though it's exhausting.

Teach a child, especially teenagers, to build a better America. Keep the laws of the land, from stop signs to the documents that you sign. When you write to your senators and congressmen to consent or to protest, share the project with your young Americans. One letter represents hundreds of other voices.

"STAND BESIDE HER AND GUIDE HER ..."

In 1776, on July 4, John Hancock led the signing of the Declaration of Independence. To those who signed, it was the most important act of their lives. Thomas Jefferson observed the day with more importance

than his birthday. John Adams said in a tribute to the day, "It is my living sentiment, and by the blessing of God, it will be my dying sentiment, Independence now and Independence Forever." Ironically, he and Jefferson died July 4, 1826, on the fiftieth anniversary of Independence Day.

"FROM THE MOUNTAINS, TO THE PRAIRIES, TO THE OCEANS WHITE WITH FOAM…"

All across America, the firecrackers sing out in remembrance of the gun powder of the Revolution. Bands play spirited and patriotic marches. People parade and politicians proclaim the freedoms and responsibilities of Americans.

The food of the day is regional — from clambakes in New England to barbecues out West. One California family remembers their New England roots by having Grandma's traditional salmon and peas. "We eat the same meal as a way of remembering where we came from and the people we love."

Each city has its special events in addition to parades, picnics, and fireworks: Missouri holds the Tom Sawyer Fence-Painting Contest. In Winston-Salem, North Carolina, there is a procession in Old Salem re-enacting the original procession in the town in 1783, the first year of peace following the American Revolution. Akron, Ohio, salutes its rich ethnic heritage with an International Festival, which features ethnic foods and crafts, along with a bike race, games, and fireworks. At Monticello, Thomas Jefferson's home in Charlottesville, Virginia, Independence Day is observed with a naturalization ceremony. Newly naturalized citizens are sworn in and honored.

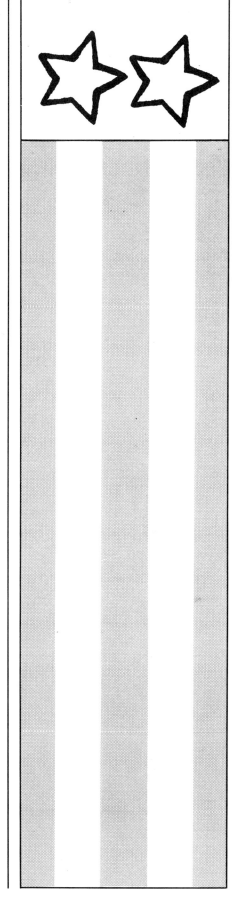

INDEPENDENCE!

"GOD BLESS AMERICA, MY HOME SWEET HOME"

Eve and Howard Hoffman's Ultimate Fourth of July Party
or
How to Celebrate the Holiday with Baseball, Contests,
Roasting Chickens, Poems, Fun, Food and Fireworks,
Just the Way John Adams Would Have Wanted It.

THE INVITATION

A poem annually invites guests to participate. "Bring baseball gloves, musical instruments, extra chairs, a Fourth of July 'presentation,' and dress in red, white, and blue." The party begins at 3:00 p.m. and continues through supper and fireworks. About 150 Fourth of July-ers, from babies to grandparents, attend.

THE SETTING

Eve and Howard live on a farm in Norcross, Georgia. The party is held in a wonderful green meadow alongside the Chattahoochee River. (Any open field or park with cooking facilities will provide a similar setting.) Flags tacked to 2 x 4s are nailed to the trees and tables; benches and extra lawn chairs are set beneath.

THE EVENTS

★ Guests arrive in the meadow in a haywagon pulled by "Big Blue," the farm tractor.

★ A Multi-Age Pick-Up Softball Game develops as the first thirty guests arrive. Captains choose teams made up of the guy in "the green cap" or "the lady in the red shirt." A terrific nine-year-old pitcher strikes out a forty-year-old slugger, and a granddad handles third base. It's a great way to mix ages and strangers.

★ A Corn Shucking Contest follows. At the sound of Eve's whistle, ten teams of six players, ranging in age from five to fifty, shuck their corn and dump it into the boiling pot. Six bales of corn for dinner are shucked in record time and sixty people share the candy corn prizes.

- ★ Paper Airplane Contests are held with left-over invitations.
- ★ Sack Racers hop off at the sound of the whistle.
- ★ There is an intense Tug-of-War for the fifteen-and-under crowd.
- ★ There is a less intense, but very enthusiastic Tug-of-War for the fifteen-and-older crowd.
- ★ A Beach Ball Blowing Contest for the little kids, ten and under, keeps them busy blowing, and later bouncing, their prized red, white, and blue balloons until dark. (Balloons resourcefully obtained free from a Radio Shack advertisement.)
- ★ Frisbees fly all afternoon and croquet balls are continuously ready to roll.

One of the secrets of this Wide World of Sports is preparation. Every item, from plastic balls to prizes, is on hand. The game schedules, which seemed effortless, have been well-planned and choreographed in advance. The attitude of the host and hostess is relaxed and contagious, and everyone from one to 100 gets into the spirit of the day.

THE FOOD

Chickens roasting on an open fire are turned all afternoon by host Hoffman and friends as they stand about watching, visiting, and cooling off with soft drinks and beer.

THE PROGRAM

At the close of supper, orators, poets, commentators, speakers, singers, and even whistlers take the stump for a two-minute discourse. Host Howard, wearing a dress shirt, knickers, and a three-cornered straw hat, introduces the politicians in attendance and calls them together for a spectacular Hot Air Contest. Each politician must blow up a balloon, seal it, and toss it into the air. A round of applause follows for the winner.

From the back of a flatbed truck, the singers, orators, and speakers give their Fourth of July "presentations." As her contribution, Cecil Busbee, daughter of Georgia's former governor George Busbee, once read part of a letter from John Adams to his wife expressing his feeling about the Fourth:

> I am apt to believe that it will be celebrated by succeeding generations as the great anniversary festival. It ought to be commemorated as the day of deliverance, by solemn acts of devotion to God Almighty. It ought to be solemnized with pomp and parade, with shows, games, sports, guns, bells, bonfires, and illuminations, from one end of this continent to the other, from this time forward forevermore.

Watermelons and the fixings for S'mores (roasted marshmallows put between squares of graham crackers and chocolate) are so good that you can't help but want s'more.

As night falls, Howard's fireworks rocket through the night air and light up the sky. It is exciting because they are so close. (It is necessary to have a permit for this event.) It is the ULTIMATE FOURTH OF JULY PARTY!!! It is just the way John Adams would have liked it. "GOD BLESS AMERICA, MY HOME SWEET HOME."

Frances Goldwasser

113

HALLOWEEN

Halloween is the children's New Year's Eve. They eat too much, they drink too much, they stay up too late, and the next morning there are hung-over monsters slumped behind millions of school desks all over America. It's a tradition! Adults also welcome the chance to join in the magic mischief-making fun.

Halloween means hallowed or holy evening because it takes place the day before All Saints Day. Old pagan customs and the Christian feast days were combined to make this eerie celebration.

Halloween is an ageless tradition at its bizarre best. The whole family can get into the act; so can the dog, Mother's new make-up, Dad's favorite trench coat, and the new guestroom sheets.

GETTING INTO THE ACT

Halloween is definitely the time to conjure up new and old customs. So pull out your Wanda the Witch or Willis the Warlock personalities and get into the act.

★ Fix spinach, okra, and liver for dinner and tell the monsters "The Devil Made You Do It!" It doesn't really matter what you're having for dinner anyway. Excited goblins never eat.

★ Wear a mask when the kids come home from school. This is a good opportunity to get in a little beauty treatment by wearing the cosmetic kind. Peel it off for them while they put on their costumes.

★ Light the house by candlelight. The neighbors will probably think you've failed to pay the power bill.

★ Hang apples on a string from the doorjamb for your wild werewolves who stalk about the house trying to put the bite on something (or someone).

★ Have a carve-in. If you are the kind of parent who saves (forgets) the pumpkin until the last minute, dash out to the supermarket for your jack-o-lantern. For the price of one giant pumpkin, you can buy a small one for each child and let each carve his own. Toast the pumpkin seeds. No matter how much salt and butter you put on them, they still taste like monster mothballs, but they are so eerily ecological.

WHAT DOES A WEREWOLF WEAR?

Deciding on costumes is a peer-group problem. Parents may have visions of Eskimos, to keep the kids warm, but the kids want to have that out-of-space look of E.T. The best way to make their Halloween tradition memorable is not to tell them what to be, but to help them "become" whatever they choose. Try on the following tips, suggestions, and directions for size.

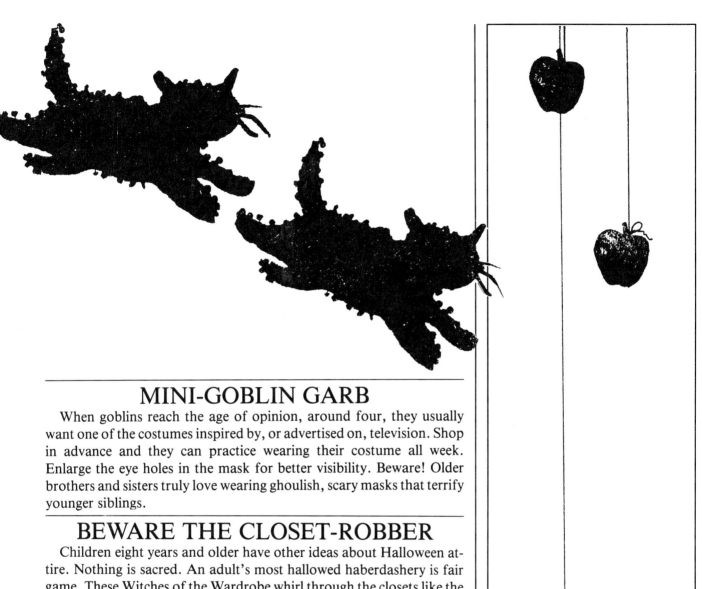

MINI-GOBLIN GARB

When goblins reach the age of opinion, around four, they usually want one of the costumes inspired by, or advertised on, television. Shop in advance and they can practice wearing their costume all week. Enlarge the eye holes in the mask for better visibility. Beware! Older brothers and sisters truly love wearing ghoulish, scary masks that terrify younger siblings.

BEWARE THE CLOSET-ROBBER

Children eight years and older have other ideas about Halloween attire. Nothing is sacred. An adult's most hallowed haberdashery is fair game. These Witches of the Wardrobe whirl through the closets like the Phantom at the Opera. If you have protective feelings about that pin-striped suit coat — ''perfect for Herman Munster'' — or your Calvin Klein trench coat — ''I've got to wear it, I'm going as a narc'' — then take your characters to the local thrift shop to search for costumes. Put together a fabulous costume for under ten dollars.

SPECIAL EFFECTS

Proteges of Steven Spielberg and Kiss get to do their thing on Halloween. Variety stores carry fangs, claws, teeth, wigs, and black tooth wax in season. They also carry Creepy Skin and Vampire Blood made by Imagineering, Inc. Moleskin is a product that is available at the drug store. It is perfect for scars and warts. Add color with paint. Waterproof magic markers can be used to draw scars. Halloween make-up kits are disappointing. *Kids Day In and Day Out* (Firestone, Simon and Schuster) offers these recipes for homebrewed blood and gore. *Facial Distortions:* Paper-mache made of Karo Syrup and Kleenex applied to the face. *Vampire Blood:* 1 cup Karo Syrup, 3 tablespoons red tempera paint (dry preferred), 4 drops red and 2 drops yellow food color. This concoction washes and wears off the face, but it stains garments.

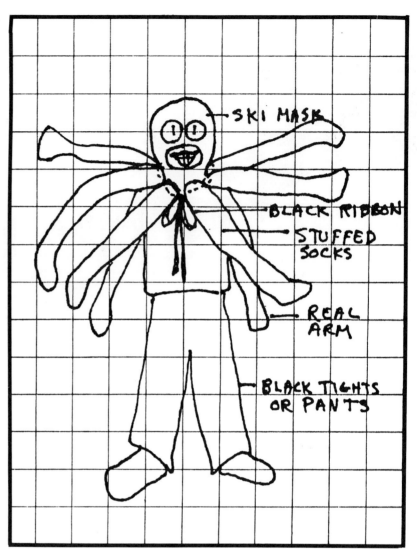

STITCHCRAFT FOR DESPERATE MONSTERS

Desperate Monsters who "haven't got a thing to wear" may appreciate these directions for implementing two do-it-yourself costumes.

SPIDER PERSON

This costume is not acceptable if your child wants to be THE Spiderman.

Supplies
black long sleeve leotard (or sweater)
black tights or pants
8 long black socks
1 yd black ribbon
safety pins
black ski hood or facsimile
stuffing (rags or newspaper)

Stuff 6 black socks tight with rags or paper. Attach each to ribbon, close together. Tie ribbon around neck. Put hood on and put last 2 socks over hands (see diagram).

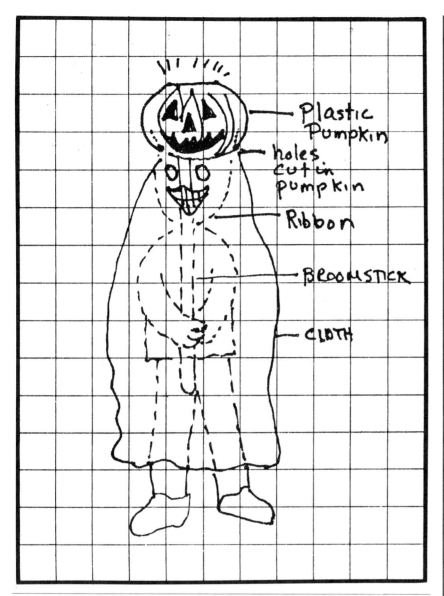

THE GREAT PUMPKIN

The Great Pumpkin has yet to appear to Charlie Brown, so your interpretation is as good as any.

Supplies

1 large plastic pumpkin
2 yds of rope or ribbon
flashlight (optional)
large white sheet or green
   or black cloth
vines or greenery

Buy a large plastic pumpkin. Punch a small hole in each side of the base. Draw the rope or ribbon through the holes (see diagram). You may need to make a large hole in the base of the pumpkin so that it sits on the head well. Put a large cloth over body. Tie the pumpkin hat on top. Make two holes in cloth. Tie a rope through the holes under the chin. Cut holes for eyes. It is possible to have vines coming out of the top of the pumpkin and hanging over the sides or to insert a lightweight, flat flashlight in the pumpkin.

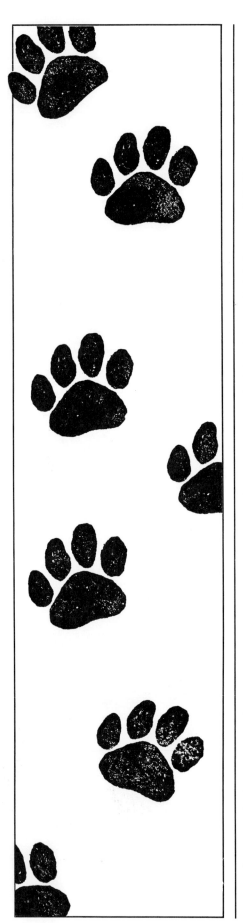

TRICK-OR-TREAT TRADITIONS

Traditions dictate that costumed children of all ages make the rounds of the neighborhood with their friends, playing pranks and getting goodies. Little children go out early and get to answer the door after dark. Big kids keep on going.

GHOST HOST

Door-answerers and Goblins alike enjoy this prank. As the T-or-T crowd approaches the door, a ghost rises from the bushes. To create a House Ghost, you will need a sheet, a balloon, twenty feet of string, and a safety pin. Blow up the balloon. Place a sheet over the balloon. Run a safety pin through the sheet and the balloon lip (outside the knot). Tie the string to the pin. Tie on a small stone for weight. Drop the balloon from the window. Hold onto string. Hide it in the bushes and wait for your first victim. Lift the "ghost" slowly and eerily up into the window. Repeat.

A CLOSE ENCOUNTER

Linda Courts and her four children travel their route each year and always make a last stop, no matter how tired they are, at the home of a neighbor. She is "about eighty-five" and they are her only callers. She awaits them and their report with cider and doughnuts.

NOT JUST KID STUFF

Halloween — it's not just for children. Adults have fabulous annual costume parties. Officials in Georgetown, in Washington, D.C., block off M and Wisconsin streets, and no one is allowed to roam the streets or the bars without a costume. The Tom Sisk family has a post-Trick-or-Treat Hallowine party. Why should the kids have all the fun?

Every year Glen Fendley gets into the spirit and the spell of Halloween. He conjures up costumes E.T. would envy. The kids in the neighborhood can't wait to make their rounds and cast their evil eyes on his current creations. His daughter Gail has carried on the family's bag of tricks, traditions, and terrific costumes. Every year she makes the Halloween "Best Dressed" list.

WHAT DO WITCHES EAT? (HALLOWEENIES)

The custom of going door-to-door begging candy, apples, and pennies goes back to the pagan New Year Feast when costumed villagers led the ghosts of the old year away from the festival table and out of town. Later, in need of a Christian rationale for the parade, the marching children were said to have agreed to pray for the souls of the dead in exchange for an offering.

Offerings abound — coins for UNICEF, raisins, sugarless gum, balloons, whistles, and pencils for the sugar-free. However, as a treat, candy wins the day.

THE DEVIL MADE ME DO IT

Beware the Calorie Count ... dare you share the loot? The listed calories are for one piece of a bag full of mini-bars:

Type of Bar	Calories
Snickers	110
Milky Way	100
Three Musketeers	80
Nestle Crunch	50
Krackle	40
Hershey Milk Chocolate	40
Mini Tootsie Roll	20
20 M&M plain	90
10 M&M peanut	120
1 lg. Peanut Butter Cup	90
6 chocolate kisses	150
10 jellybeans	100
5 candy corns	45
1 licorice twist	30

Wash the whole bag down with a Tab!

WITCHES' RICHES

The days of goblins who soap windows, turn over outhouses, and trim the trees with toilet paper seem to have passed. There is, however, the horror of poisoned candy or razor blades in apples conjured up by sick minds. This inspired the P.T.A. in Central Islip, New York, to offer an alternative to Halloween candy. They sell 5¢ coupons to families to hand out on Halloween. The coupons are redeemable at variety stores, local banks, the school lunchroom, or the neighborhood supermarket. Forty thousand coupons sold in 1980.

SUPERSTITIONS

Halloween is superstition prime-time. Superstitions are, of course, ridiculous. Everyone knows that knocking on wood and saying "God bless you" when you sneeze are silly traditions. But why take chances, and why not pass on these binding "crazy family traditions" just as they were passed to you. Here are some modern interpretations of ancient omens.

THE SPILLED SALT OMEN

Did you ever get through one meal without someone spilling salt (and milk and peas, etc.) without a fight ensuing within seconds? You may think a fight would have occurred anyway, but it WAS the salt.

DON'T WALK UNDER THE LADDER

All you have to do is drag the ladder out of the garage and up the drive, then maneuver it under the dirty windows, and every male of any age in the house will scream, "Bad omen, bad omen," and start running in all directions.

DON'T GET UP ON THE
WRONG SIDE OF THE BED

Are the ancients kidding? Only kids who float all night in circular water beds don't get up grouchy.

SPITTING FOR LUCK OMEN

There are also Good Luck Superstitions that wind their weird way into your home such as the Spitting for Luck Omen. It is difficult to find a young, average American male under (or over) fifteen who doesn't practice this superstition.

THE FOUR LEAF CLOVER IS GOOD LUCK

Don't bet on it. If your child has gotten mixed up with four leaf clovers, chances are that this urban child has joined the 4-H Club and wants you to drive him every Wednesday and Friday to his new bucolic bag.

WEAR YOUR CLOTHING INSIDE OUT

It is also supposed to be good luck. No wonder children survive so successfully. Have you ever seen one who went out anywhere with everything right side out?

Don't let the mood and the spirit of this holiday intimidate you. Use it to your own advantage. Create your own superstitions. Tell your apprentice witch that if she doesn't eat her spinach, she will grow warts on her dimples when she grows up. And tell your little Frankenstein that if he doesn't shake hands with adults and look them in the eye, his fingers will fall off one at a time when he's over thirty. Kids love it when the hag who's stirring the boiling pot in the kitchen gets in the mood of their holiday.

THE LEGEND OF
JACK-O'-LANTERN —
PASS IT ON!

The Irish brought Jack-O'-Lantern to America. Jack was a legendary, stingy drunkard. He tricked the Devil into climbing an apple tree for a juicy apple and then quickly cut the sign of the cross into the tree trunk, preventing the Devil from coming down. Jack made the Devil swear that he wouldn't come after his soul in any way. The Devil promised. However, this did not prevent Jack from dying. When he arrived at the gates of heaven, he was turned away because he was a stingy, mean drunk. Desperate for a resting place, he went to the Devil. The Devil, true to his word, turned him away. "But where can I go?" pleaded Jack. "Back where you come from," spoke the Devil. The night was dark and the way was long, and the Devil tossed him a lighted coal from the fire of Hell. Jack, who was eating a turnip at the time, placed the coal inside and used it to light his way. Since that day, he has traveled the world over with his Jack-O'-Lantern in search of a place to rest. Irish children carved out turnips and potatoes to light the night on Halloween. When the Irish came to America in great numbers in the 1840s, they found that a pumpkin made an even better lantern, and so this "American" tradition came to be.

123

THANKSGIVING DAY

Today, as in 1621, the tradition of giving thanks is mixed with family, food, and football.

The first American Thanksgiving was a three-day celebration which began with breakfast for ninety-two people. It was served on benches out in the yard and, as a surprise for the Pilgrims, the Indians turned up with the first bowl of popcorn. Right there is reason enough to give thanks. No matter what this traditional day holds in store, you can be thankful that you don't have ninety-two people coming to an outdoor breakfast or staying over for a three-day feast.

And if your turkey dinner is sandwiched between football games, don't despair. Sports are part of the tradition of the day. At the original feast, the game was stool ball (a kind of croquet) and ninety Wanponag braves "took on" the settlers in track and field events.

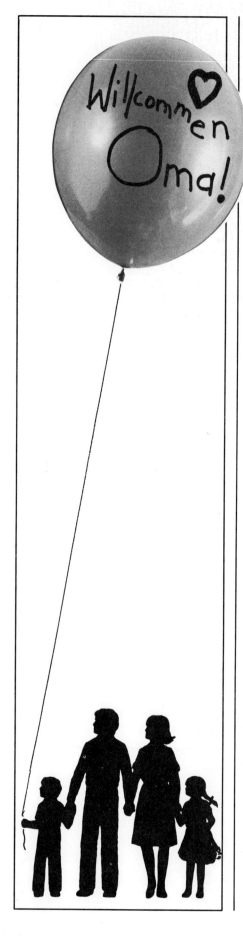

WE GATHER TOGETHER TO ASK THE LORD'S BLESSING (or Songs of Thanksgiving)

Each Pilgrim Father and every Indian Mother has every right to look at their tribe and give thanks that the brave little band has weathered another year; withstood their storms; built their foundations; planted, nurtured and harvested their crops.

Take time to take stock of what each person has toiled to produce, whether it is better grades, kicking a soccer goal, getting a raise, learning to read, or turning out a family "with no cavities."

GIVING THANKS

Prayers and songs of Thanksgiving can take many forms. The tradition of joining hands around the dinner table has a special warm feeling.

★ Begin the meal with the usual mealtime grace, symbolizing continued appreciation for God's blessings.

★ Go around the table, starting with the leader, and say, "I am thankful for _____," followed by the next person who adds, "For _____." Children are encouraged to say two things, one tangible and one intangible.

★ Try a Thanksgiving version of the game "Grandmother's Trunk." The first person, Uncle Bob, says, "I am thankful for good health." Number 2, Jim, says, "I'm thankful for Uncle Bob's health and my girlfriend, Jane." Number 3, Sally, says, "I am thankful for Uncle Bob's health, Jim's girlfriend, Jane, and my new bicycle." This is a fun, funny icebreaker for family sharing.

★ The Savitt family in Hartford, Connecticut, begins every family gathering by holding hands and singing, "I've Got the Joy, Joy, Joy Down in My Heart" and "The More We Are Together." This tradition has been known to take place even in public restaurants, albeit at a whisper.

Thanksgiving is an original "born and bred in America" holiday. Give recognition to the country of its origin, to its people, and its leaders. Give your Thanksgiving meal a truly glorious ending by joining hands and singing "God Bless America."

Macy's Thanksgiving Day Parade

127

danny

carole

greg

jilly

THE FEAST

"Breaking bread" together is a traditional bonding experience. The meal is the center of this holiday. Turkey and dressing, cranberries, sweet potatoes, and pumpkin pie make for the dinner of record.

Some celebrants follow the menu and early recipes exactly; some have variations on the theme. Others are influenced by their family's place of origin. With some, the meal is a team effort; but always, the table should be beautiful.

SET THE TABLE "CON AMORE" — WITH LOVE

The gathering of the clan at the holiday table is the center of the celebration. A beautiful table is a sign of welcome and shows appreciation for each guest. Designer Penny Goldwasser sets her table based on the Danish proverb "First the flowers — then the food."

Color excites the palate. Flowers, fruit, vegetables, and green leaves are nature's gift to the Thanksgiving table. Children's handmade turkeys or other art work can be incorporated into the centerpiece. Low votive candles cast a warm and flattering glow on the guests.

Place cards unify and personalize the table. They become an instant conversation piece and a favor for the guests.

★ Mark each place with a small framed photo of the guest.
★ Personalize glass mugs for each guest with nail polish or model airplane paint.
★ Give small personalized note pads as a place favor.
★ Challenge guests to find themselves in descriptive poems written as place cards.
★ Tie children's handmade turkeys or place cards to a tiny flower basket for favors.
★ Give mini-kaleidoscopes as fabulous favors and conversation-makers.
★ Shirley Anderson collects shells. She paints her guests' names on them and uses them for Thanksgiving or whenever they come to dinner.

ETHNIC AMERICAN MENUS

Actress-director Geraldine Fitzgerald has a traditional meal. Her children like it exactly as it is in their story books, never anything different. There is always turkey, real cranberries, and sweet potato pie with meringue topping. Ms. Fitzgerald comes from Ireland where they do not celebrate Thanksgiving. She says her own Thanksgiving dish would be Irish Stew.

Photographer Inge Morath and her husband, playwright Arthur Miller, are vegetarians. She usually creates a "pretend turkey" out of vegetables — a pièce montée. She uses a loaf of bread as a base and arranges cold, cooked and raw vegetables on top, like a painting. Pieces of avocado make beautiful wings. It looks more like a live turkey than a dead one. With it, she serves the usual American sweet potatoes and cranberry sauce along with her own Austrian cake.

Author I.B. Singer is also a vegetarian. He is against killing any creature on this or any other day. He likes the annual national celebration of gratitude but adds, "I think that every human being should have a minute every day to say they are grateful."

With Thanksgiving!

Frances Goldwasser

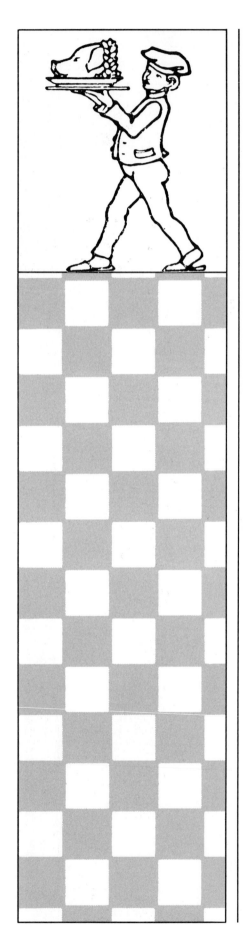

SHARING THE LOAD

Dancer-choreographer Jacque d'Amboise celebrates the holiday with two other families. They rotate houses and each year the host family gets the turkey, another brings the vegetables, the other brings the desserts.

In the Fendley family, and in many others, each branch of the clan traditionally brings a dish to the gathering. Young adults who have moved out and are working are not required to bring a dish, but when one of them marries, they become "a pot-carrying member of the family." This is a family rite of passage for newlyweds.

HASSLE-FREE THANKSGIVING

For some, cooking is a relaxing, creative experience. For others, it is the pits. It leaves them drained of any joy for the celebration. Professional caterers can handle the hassle. One of the favorite traditions of the John Walley family is the annual trip to Morrison's cafeteria on Thursday morning to stand in line with all the other heat-and-eat cooks who gratefully await their turkey, dressing, gravy and pecan pies. When compliments come and recipes are requested, he proudly says, "Oh, thank you, I'm so glad you liked it." The urge for the recipe will usually get lost in the shuffle, and any fake cook can be thankful for that.

Amy Marmonstein is always in the Morrison's line. She goes to her sister's house for the holiday meal, but she always gets a turkey for the family weekend. Her comment: "What's Thanksgiving without leftovers?"

CHOCOLATE TURKEY

The Bradbury family dessert is a Baskin and Robbins Ice Cream Turkey. The body is an oval ice cream mold. The legs are chocolate scoops attached to the body and topped with sugar cones. The Bradbury turkey has four legs, one for each grandchild.

Catch the Ice Cream Turkey at Baskin-Robbins.

ACTIVITIES

Children are the bearers of the flame. When they grow up, it will fall to them to carry on the family traditions. The activities that surround the Thanksgiving meal provide more fun for young people than the too-long, too-many-vegetables meal.

Participation in the day's other activities prevents boredom and creates a positive attitude toward the holiday.

THE ANNUAL THANKSIVING DAY PARADE

The Macy's Thanksgiving Day Parade is a great American tradition. Artist Claes Oldenburg used the giant balloon creations as inspirations for his soft sculptures. Advertising executives Lisa and Thos Paine have Thanksgiving breakfast while they watch the parade assemble beneath their window on New York's West Side. For millions of other T.V.-viewing Americans, the Thanksgiving Day Parade traditionally begins this celebration.

NOTHING SPELLS LOVIN'
LIKE SOMETHING FROM THE OVEN

For the Crammond family, the holiday begins on Thanksgiving eve with their tradition of sharing home-baked bread and sweet butter. The tradition began as a treat for all the small neighborhood children at 7:30 p.m. and became a teenage favorite. No beer, no dancing, just the wonderful taste and aroma of homemade bread and butter.

HOME FOR THE HOLIDAYS

In Boston, everyone in the Davis household goes to the airport to greet incoming family members. There is an air of excitement on this busiest of all holidays. Hugging and kissing and walking to the baggage claim holding hands gives the family WFF. Airline personnel really gear up to enhance the holiday spirit. Delta Air Lines is especially conscious of holiday sensitivies. It is their tradition to serve turkey and all the trimmings to passengers flying their routes on Turkey Day.

FAMILY K-P

The Jones family shares the load if family and friends are coming for the holiday.

They make a rotating job list which includes jobs for all ages and post the names of those who share the jobs at each shift. Cousins are put together by ages. Adults are mixed together by sex. It's fun to find out who has to do what with whom. Everyone gets one "freebie."
Jobs include:
★ Set table
★ Clear table
★ Clean up den
★ Take trash out
★ Make salad
★ Load dishwasher
★ Unload dishwasher and put away ("This results in a month-long family scavenger hunt after everyone leaves," say the Joneses.)
★ Freebie

131

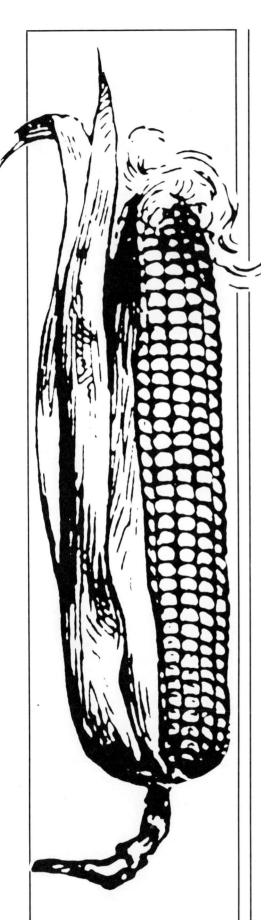

The chart takes care of the "guilt and gripe" segment of the weekend. There's no guilt by the guests for not doing more for the hostess; no gripes by the hostess for having too much to do.

ALONE FOR THE HOLIDAYS

Consumer activist Ralph Nader says he has turkey at his desk and spends the day working on making our Constitution apply to our nation's policies. He is made of tough stuff.

Holidays require planning ahead. One woman whose children spend the holiday with her husband usually visits family or friends out of town. She says, "I pitch in and I'm an extra pair of hands at a busy time. I appreciate the change of scene from what would be a very lonely home."

HOMETOWN ACTIVITIES

Take a thermos of hot chocolate to a Thanksgiving morning activity. Attend a hometown football game, a charity foot race, or one of America's big parades. Or gather around the T.V. for a breakfast of popcorn and watch the Macy's Thanksgiving Day Parade.

CARVE-IN

The highlight of the Savitt-Nathanson Thanksgiving dinner is the Turkey Carving Contest. There is a turkey on each end of the table. The contest pits Uncle Al, representing the Nathanson clan, against Uncle Sidney for the Savitt side of the family. The winner is the fastest carver. Neatness counts!

AUDIO AND VIDEO

Photos are the order of the day. Take some informal shots in the kitchen, and do your own version of the famous Norman Rockwell Thanksgiving illustration. Put a mike in the centerpiece and tape-record the meal. Play it back after dinner and send it on to an absent family member. If you have video equipment, record the "turkeys" and "hams" at your house in action.

OPEN DOOR POLICY

Share your Thanksgiving spirit and meal with a foreign student anxious for a taste of this American tradition. Locate students through area colleges or the bureau of international visitors.

CLOSING THE GENERATION GAP

All family gatherings can span the widest range of ages and interests and can be the "gappiest" part of the Generation Gap. Capitalize on this "gap." Take advantage of the rich reserves of remembrances at the table by having each person in turn recall his favorite pet, his favorite radio or T.V. show, his nickname, the origin of his name, his favorite or least favorite teacher, his best friend as a twelve-year-old, and his most thankful Thanksgiving. Young family members learn funny and interesting things about Grandpa's nickname or how he got his first bike, and Aunt Mary shares a new feeling towards Lee when she discovers that they both like "Pong." The family is in for a generous helping of sharing and comparing.

THIS IS YOUR LIFE

The sad, funny, ordinary, and remarkable childhood memories of grandparents, parents and aunts, uncles and children are great connectors. William Zinnerman, a long-time journalist and father of an elementary school student, has written *How to Tape Instant Oral Biographies*. The book looks like a reporter's note pad and is available for $5.95. Mr. Zinnerman has an equation: "Grandchild plus tape recorder equals living history." The book is a paperback guide to capturing and preserving the life stories of relatives and friends by using standard interviewing techniques.

Every child seven and up knows how to be a T.V. reporter. Send him off with a tape recorder, a relative, and a set of questions and then play it back for the family. The second grade at Hunter Elementary School used this technique as an activity for Grandparents' Day at the school. Try the following questions:

★ What is your full name?
★ Do you know what it means?
★ What was your life like when you were my age?
★ What were your parents like?
★ Who were your favorite relatives and why?
★ Did you have any brothers and sisters and where were you in the family?
★ What did you look like when you were my age?
★ Did you have a nickname? How did you get it?
★ What is your happiest memory as a child? Saddest?
★ What was it like to be a teenager?
★ How did you meet your mate?

This project works best if both parties are prepared. Let the child practice and become familiar with the tape recorder and inform the interviewee in advance, if possible. The reporter should know that his guest might be shy and needs to be reassured that the interview is very important to him.

SNAP CRACKLE POP-CORN

Popcorn was a surprise gift for the Pilgrims at the first Thanksgiving dinner. According to legend, popcorn was discovered in the fifteenth century when a group of teenage American Indians threw some corn cobs on the campfire. Snap, Crackle, and Pop-Corn was born! Make popcorn part of your Thanksgiving tradition:

★ Use it as part of the holiday table decorations. In 1519 while exploring Mexico, Cortez found the Aztecs wearing popcorn in their ceremonial headdresses. It can be used as decoration by stringing it with cranberries or sprinkling it around the centerpiece of the table.
★ Do as the colonists did — use popcorn as croutons in soup.
★ Shake popcorn in a bag of brown sugar and cinnamon, then mix it in fruit salad.
★ Mix popcorn with melted chocolate chips, then drop spoonfuls on waxed paper to harden as candy.

133

RELIGIOUS HOLIDAYS

Religious holidays are celebrated world-wide. These holidays connect observers in a tradition that is larger than family. The family's retelling of the birth of the baby Jesus or the Exodus from Egypt provides an opportunity for the stories of the faith to be passed from generation to generation. The continuity of religious celebrations is a comforting connection in a sometimes lonely world.

CHRISTMAS

Christmas celebrates the birth of Christ with the message of peace on earth, goodwill toward men. Although the commercialization of this holiday is frustrating to many, the celebration gives a warm glow at a cold time of the year. Neighbors speak, old friends get in touch, and strangers share a greeting.

People in a hundred languages sing the joys of Christmas and share their respective countries' traditions. Austria gave us "Silent Night" and other beautiful carols. England contributed the mistletoe ball, and Germany's gift was the tree. These traditions, which are as old as Bethlehem, continue to be celebrated with fresh and innovative ideas.

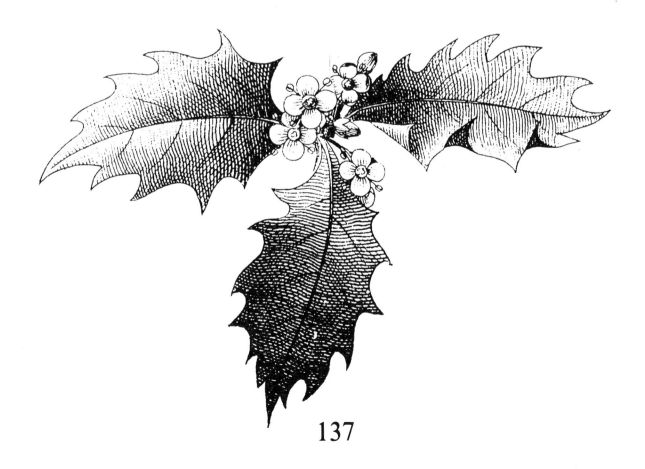

137

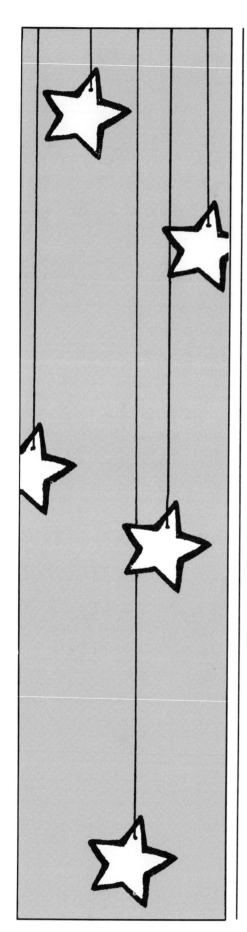

25 CHRISTMAS IDEAS

Food and festivities bring family and friends together. Large families refresh and renew their rituals, and singles and small families create new customs and celebrations. Newlyweds work through years of "his" and "her" traditions to create their customs. Unwrap the following twenty-five ideas for Christmas parties, presents, and celebrations and try them on for size.

LIGHT UP THE LIFE
OF YOUR OWN CHRISTMAS STAR

Dedicate a star to someone you think is heavenly. This star can be named for them, permanently registered at the International Star Registry, and then copyrighted at the Library of Congress for $30. Their star will shine like Orion's for millions of years as a reminder of this out-of-this-world gift. Write the International Star Registry, 1821 Willow Rd., Northfield, Illinois 60093; or phone 1-800-323-0766 for further information. For another star idea, do as designers Yasushi and Kiyoko Suzuki did. They suspended silver stars on nylon thread from the ceiling in the alcove above their tree.

TREES WITH A TAX-FREE TAG

Henrietta Egleston Hospital for Children is one of the finest hospitals of its kind in the country. The Festival of Trees is an annual Christmas event which benefits this hospital. Outstanding designers decorate the trees, and thousands pay a small fee to see these beautifully executed ideas. Individuals or companies then bid on the trees, and at the end of the festival, around December 13, each tree goes to the highest bidder for his home or office. Both the donors and the hospital enjoy a better and brighter Christmas.

A PRE-PACKAGE PRESENT

Anne Goodsell delivers Christmas gift-wrapping supply baskets in early December. Bright red and green baskets from the Farmers' Market are filled with labels and tape, ornament hangers, two-way scotch tape, gift tags, bows, a small bottle of glue. The baskets also include Tums, Certs, aspirin, hand lotion, and a split of champagne. It's a great set-up and gets Christmas wrappers in the spirits.

A MERRY MINGLE FOR SINGLES

If you are single and short on funds, create a Dutch celebration and invite friends to B.Y.O. — bring your own dish and bring your own spirits. As the host, provide an abundance of candles in different shapes or in a combination of candlesticks, or use a mass of votive cups. Light up the tree and the party place. Create a Christmas glow, a warmth, and a memory.

SILENT SANTA GIFTS

In the Burchfield family, each member draws a name, and for one week before Christmas he or she becomes that person's Silent Secret Santa. They provide small thoughts and kindnesses, taking great care not to be discovered. They leave a mint on the pillow, straighten shoes in the closet, and always leave a sign that says, "With love, S.S.S."

BRIGHT MEMORIES

A small church has a large memorial poinsettia tree near the altar each Christmas. A scaffold is erected near the pulpit to hold gift pots of brilliant red poinsettias placed in remembrance of a friend or family member. It is a magnificent church tree, ablaze with personal memories.

SHARE THE SPIRIT

Flo Bernard had a Christmas benefit party and spread the spirit of the season beyond her own circle of friends. She checked with local charities and emergency relief organizations for information on the kind of help they needed. She chose the Girls' Club and on the party invitation asked the guests to bring a donation of books, clothes, cosmetics, sports equipment, etc. The guests enjoyed the party, the sense of shared participation, and the fact that the hostess handled the delivery. This annual party with a purpose is a real celebration.

DONATION INNOVATION

The donation given by a favorite aunt to the Children's Fund in the name of her nieces and nephews not only gives her small relatives the joy of seeing their names in the paper, but also provides an awareness that there are needs greater than their own. The fund and the family all benefit.

Glo ri a in excelsis

De o.
BETHLEHEM, CONN.
The
CHRISTMAS TOWN

I DON'T VANT TO BE ALONE

If you are alone at Christmas, contact a church or other organization and tell them you are interested in sharing your Christmas with others. This is not always easy, but it can be an adventure.

When your guest arrives, treat him/her like family and lovingly put him to work setting the table or adding last-minute ornaments to the tree. Don't do everything before the guest gets there. Plan organized confusion and the noise and clatter of activities will fill the quiet pauses. Cook the meal together. Nothing is more binding than creating a mess with someone else.

THE DESK SET FOR CHRISTMAS DAY

Take a poll of office workers and see who will be alone for Christmas Day. Have a Brunch with a Punch. Draw names for gifts, set a dollar amount, and then wrap the gift with cut-outs from company annual reports, office newsletters, memos, or trade magazines.

CHRISTMAS BREAKFAST BASKETS

The Wright family decorates Christmas breakfast baskets with festive cloths for their special friends. Each basket is filled with homemade banana bread or store-bought croissants, country jams, sweet butter, sausages, and packages of specially brewed hot chocolate or coffee mixes with tags that read, "Just add water or milk." They are delivered on Christmas Eve afternoon and usually call for a lingering chat and Christmas spirits.

HARK, THE NEIGHBORHOOD ANGELS SING

Tennis instructor Claudine Lindberg grew up in New Jersey with a tradition of Christmas caroling with the kids in the neighborhood. Today, she and her husband, their three children, the kids on the soccer teams she coaches, and all of their friends who don't have family in town carry on the tradition.

"I put notes in the neighbors' mailboxes asking them to leave their lights on if they will be home the night we are caroling. We still use the songbooks my kids made when they were little. It's really a pick-up singing group—no practice—but everybody loves the harmony of being together."

A FAMILY CLASSIC

McCall's featured this classic Christmas gift:

John Hallagan, of Milwaukee, Wisconsin, wanted to give his parents a Christmas present to remember, so he asked his eleven brothers and sisters to write about what it means to be a member of the Hallagan family. The result was "The Family Classics," a collection of funny stories and happy memories, illustrated with photographs of the authors from infancy to adulthood. Contributions ranged from one-page essays by some of the younger children to a ten-page play. As more of the Hallagans get married and have their own children, the "Classics" — which now fills four photograph albums — will be updated with essays from the newest family members.

the Christmas town
BETHLEHEM, CONN.

"THE CHRISTMAS TOWN"

BETHLEHEM
CONNECTICUT

BETHLEHEM, CONN.
THE
CHRISTMAS TOWN

CHRISTMAS SNOWBALLS

After all of the Christmas presents have been unwrapped and there is a mound of paper strewn about, make snowballs. Ask everyone to wad the paper into snowballs and send the super-excited young or young at heart outside for a snowball bout. Enjoy the clean scene.

PACKAGING WITH PANACHE

Packaging is as important as the present. Sometimes it's not the bauble but the box.

A Tiffany box speaks class, no matter what the contents. "Favorite aunts, Amy and Rae, love knowing that I thought of them while shopping there," says Mickie Jordon. The box gives a touch of glamour to any gift.

HAVE YOURSELF
A MERRY LITTLE CHRISTMAS

Terry Alexander grew up in San Francisco, and going to see the movie "Meet Me in St. Louis" was a Christmas tradition in his family. The family moved and the movie wasn't shown in their new locale. The tradition slowly disappeared but not the memory or the Christmas celebration. "In our family, I am in charge of Christmas," Terry said. "Last year it was Victorian. There were layered tablecloths, lace and silver. After dinner, the family gift was the surprise of an at-home showing of 'our' movie. There wasn't a dry eye."

AND IT CAME TO PASS

Michael and Donna Egan have six children and a spirited Christmas season. On Christmas Eve, they bring that spirit into focus with their tradition of having everybody read a favorite selection. The tradition began when their youngest child was about eleven and "it was time for a more grown-up Christmas tradition."

Michael begins by reading the passage in Luke about the birth of the Christ Child. Individual selections about Christmas or otherwise come from short stories, poems, or books. Newlyweds and in-laws also read. "Everybody gets very busy thumbing through books right before Christmas Eve," Donna commented, adding, "Sometimes I give them a little help with their choices."

CHRISTMAS REUNION

Christmas is a time of family reunions, especially for the eight Conley children of Texas. "Each year, we gather with our mother, our twenty-four children, an increasing number of grandchildren and great-grandchildren, aunts, uncles, formers, ex's, in-laws, friends, and foes for a day of food, fun, and fellowship for seven to seventy-five people."

An invitation with a theme gives all the information for the games, gifts, dress, and program. "Being the only family members in Georgia, we wanted to have a special reunion," said Marceline Winn. "Ours was the Conley Christmas Olympics. We had prizes for the first three families who arrived. Then we had the Lighting of the Olympic Flame (the Christmas tree), relays, races, and an egg-throwing contest between the families of the eight children. There were awards for the most unusual or the funniest Olympic-wear. The responsibility for the meal is shared, special recognition of our mother is always given, and then everybody over twelve is 'invited' to clean up.''

O LITTLE TOWN OF BETHLEHEM

The town of Bethlehem, Connecticut, has a tradition that it shares with the world. It began in 1938 when Postmaster Earl Johnson designed a rubber stamp with a Christmas greeting to decorate his own Christmas mail. The idea was adopted by the town and became a tradition. Every year there is a new design with the greeting, *A Merry Christmas from Bethlehem, Connecticut, The Christmas Town.*

Each December all of the stamps are set out and people come with their packages and decorate the mail with the Christmas designs. If you would like to share in this tradition you may send your cards to: The Postmaster, Bethlehem, Connecticut 06751. This is the procedure: Address and seal your cards. Affix postage stamps on each card. The Christmas stamps are decorative cachets, they are not postage. Enclose a letter in the package with your cards requesting that they be stamped with the annual seal and mailed from Bethlehem. The town is generous in this effort, in the true Christmas spirit.

BETHLEHEM, CONN. THE CHRISTMAS TOWN

OLD BETHLEM MUSEUM
BETHLEHEM, CONN.

BETHLEHEM, CONN.

The Christmas Town

BETHLEHEM CONNECTICUT

BINGO AND BIRTHDAY CAKE

Gertrude Smith's Christmas Eve is full of family gifts, giggling, and celebrating. "We always start the evening with Bingo. It's the great equalizer for little ones, teens, grown-ups and grandparents. It's the time for cocktails and Cokes followed by the gift-giving, trading, and trying on. Christmas Eve dinner is a tradition and so is the picture of the children we take after dinner when they light the cake and sing 'Happy Birthday' to Jesus."

A VISIT FROM ST. NICK

Save your money all year and give yourself the gift of a getaway at Christmas.

Go on a Christmas Eve trip to a nearby inn with a friend. Decorations, dinner, and a date — that's a Christmas delight.

A writer for *Cosmopolitan* who was overweight gave herself a trip to a spa during Christmas week. She lost weight and gained a merrier Christmas.

MYSTERY GIFT

This idea started when Willa Drummond couldn't remember how many Christmas gifts she had bought for each of her three children. Had she bought too much for one, not enough for another? Heaven forbid the gifts shouldn't be even! She wrapped one nice present suitable for either sex and put it under the tree to give the giftee with the short stack. It was marked Santa Special-Mystery Gift. It caused so much attention, anticipation, and excitement that it became a tradition. Each year all four family members keep their eye on the mystery gift, hoping to be The One to get it.

UNWRAPPING OF GIFTS

The unwrapping of gifts can be a glorious scene of paper and presents in a shared adventure. In the Alexander family, the youngest person delivers all the gifts. Each person takes turns opening a gift while the rest of the family makes wild guesses, speculates, or tries to make sight-unseen trades. Shared anticipation doubles the pleasure, doubles the fun. Each gift gets to center stage, and notes for Christmas thank-you notes are noted.

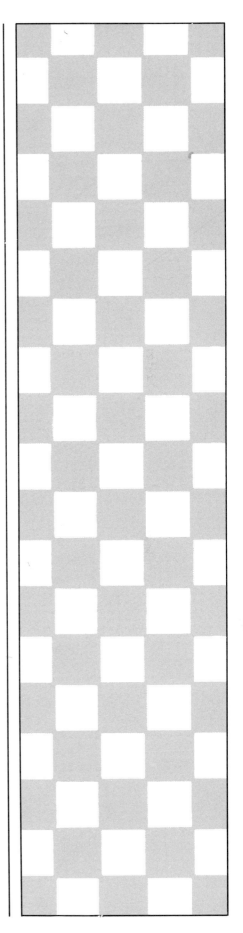

THE MISTLETOE SHOOT

Christmas parties that are a mixture of all ages add to the spirit of the holiday. Each Christmas for eleven years, Dutton and Sandy Morehouse have had their Annual Morehouse Family Shoot. They invite friends to bring their parents, grandparents, teens, tots and other friends. Every year more friends are invited to the farm party and more "events" are added. Pony rides, treasure hunts, tug-of-war, and earth ball games are great mixers. Everyone gets in on the mistletoe shoot. Mistletoe grows on the trunks and branches of various tall trees. It takes a good eye and a steady hand to bring down this prized kissing branch.

I'LL BE HOME FOR CHRISTMAS

"I'll Be Home for Christmas" is not just a sentimental song, but a fact of life for the Knox family of Thomson, Georgia. "Our Christmas Eve tradition is an unbroken chain. Since the early 1930s, spanning five generations, open-heart surgery, car wrecks, or other family traumas, our family continues to celebrate Christmas Eve at the ancestral home," Margaret Knox boasted.

"The Knox men still gather early in the evening in a back room for a glass or two of Christmas cheer. A young Knox male has 'come of age' when he is permitted to join this group with perhaps a special toast or a word of welcome.

"The dinner is a masterpiece of old family recipes. One dare not suggest that scalloped oysters be replaced by another dish or that the turkey dressing be altered by a single herb," she continued.

"When the last family member has arrived from near and far, the family circle is again formed with a word of welcome and this prayer:

Especially thankful are we tonight for those who established this home, for those who lived in it but have gone along their way, for those who maintain it as an anchor of family unity to which we all cling, and for all these bright and healthy youngsters with their wonderful futures stretched years ahead."

146

TREE TRIMMING

The Cunningham family has a special ornament for each member of the family. When each arrives for the holiday, his ornament goes on the tree.

Another family saves chicken wishbones all year and sprays them white. Visitors at Christmas are invited to take a bone, make a wish, and tie their "wish" on the tree.

When Lynn Sitler and her brother were born, their parents started a Christmas tradition by adding an ornament for their tree with each child's name and the date. "Now that we are grown and away from home, having our own ornaments from the family tree makes me feel less homesick," said Lynn. "It is the little things that parents do that show they love you, and I love this tradition."

GIFT WRAPPING — DRESS FOR SUCCESS

★ Wrap your gifts distinctively to add luster to the gift and to honor the receiver with this extra care.

★ Use baskets for consumable goodies. The basket is the lasting gift. A fabulous fabric with pinked edges can be used in the basket as both a liner and a dash of color.

★ Designer Penny Goldwasser adds a sprig of greenery under the package bow, which is usually plum or hot pink.

★ Adair Sisk gives her family gifts uniquely wrapped into a Christmas ball. The gifts can be anything from chocolate candies and baseball cards to more elaborate jewelry or plane tickets for a Christmas trip. The balls are made by winding crepe paper or wrapping paper streamers around the fun and fancy items spaced throughout the ball. Unwrapping these gifts is half the fun.

★ Use recycled newspaper as gift wrap for a graphic look. Accent with bright red ribbon. The *Wall Street Journal* or foreign newspapers add special style.

★ Fabric scarves, napkins, or distinctive fabric scraps add a gift to the gift.

★ Copy the English. Give a finished look to plants in plastic pots. A square of fabric wrapped around the plastic pot with an elastic band and secured at the roots adds a collar and a touch of class to the plant.

★ Add to the wrap Crazy Shoe String "ribbon," silk flowers, colored high tech paper clips, candy treats, or a cookie iced with the name of the receiver.

★ Brighten the postman's day. Decorate the mailing carton with felt tip marker designs.

★ Canned gifts can be sent through the mail. Many shopping malls have a canning machine. Anything from homemade bonbons to a personalized T-shirt can be put into the cans which are vacuum-sealed. Add a colorful label of your own.

EASTER

Easter celebrates the rebirth of Christ and the renewal of nature. It is the most important holiday in the Christian religion and calls for rejoicing, celebrating, and singing.

Karen Bacon is an "event maker." In her business, she has planned major celebrations for the city of New York, including the Great Egg Event for the Bronx Zoo. It is a weekend of parades, pageants, egg-decorating, chicken-hatchings, and egg-rolling activities. "I think celebrations are something people need," Ms. Bacon said, "especially now, in the time of television. People need times when they can physically participate and do things together."

FAITH

HOPE

CHARITY

JOY!

CELEBRATE WITH A SPIRIT THAT'S ALIVE

Celebrate Easter or Passover with a spirit that is alive and singing.

Bring an abundance of glorious flowers and budding branches into the house. Make paper flowers to decorate holiday tables.

Let each person bring his gift to the day. Some of the family can prepare part of the meal as their contribution. The older children can write different psalms or favorite verses to be put on napkins for everyone to read aloud. Teenagers or camera buffs can use their imaginations to show the rebirth of spring through a nature slide show. The six-year-old can bring his newly found ability to whistle or snap his fingers.

Let someone tell the Easter or Passover story in "now" language, as if he were a network reporter covering the event.

"Make a joyful noise unto the Lord" — make a loud noise with today's music. Have a solo performance on instruments currently being played. Give toy harmonicas as table favors. Pre-tape songs for the whole day, such as "Jesus Christ Superstar," "Godspell," "What the World Needs Now," "When the Saints Go Marching In," or "Oh Happy Day."

As a treat after the holiday meal, invite everybody outside to fly kites. Give kites or have a wide assortment of colored paper and magic markers, clay or wire, and let each person create his own.

Buy a copy of *Catch the New Wind* by Marilee Zdnenek and Marge Champion. This book has fresh and stimulating ideas for "now" worship. It represents an effervescent faith and begins, "May the Holy Spirit zap you until you tingle with joy."

AS A TOKEN

On Palm Sunday at the Cathedral of Christ the King, it is traditional to give each member of the congregation a small nail as a reminder of the events leading up to the Easter celebration. Each member carries it in his/her pocket or keeps it in a prominent place to remind him of the

Last Supper, the betrayal of Christ by Judas, and the Crucifixion. It is an outward and visible symbol of the inward and spiritual meaning of Easter.

ANIMAL FARM

Easter celebrates the rebirth of nature. Nothing is more symbolic or sensational than baby chicks, ducks, or rabbits. Katie Breen of the Humane Society recommends that if an animal is part of your Easter tradition, it should be the cuddly, soft, and stuffed kind. Stuffed animals can survive the patting, petting, and constant handling that may kill live animals.

Breeding pets are raised with controlled temperature, light, and food. They need these conditions to thrive. Ms. Breen recommends a rabbit if a pet is a priority. They can be leashed and litter trained!

THE HUNT IS ON

It rained for the first three years Adair Oliver's children were old enough for an Easter Egg Hunt, so the eggs were hidden inside the house. They were hidden under sofa pillows, behind plant leaves, and inside magazine racks. It became an easy, rain-proof, and unusual tradition. As the children grew older and Easter trips became part of the spring vacation, the eggs continued to be hidden on the inside of motel and hotel rooms. Adair commented, "It's much more comfortable running around the inside of the motel room in my nightie hiding eggs than it would have been outside. Somehow my vision of Easter does not include a thirty-eight-year-old woman, in sleepwear, with Easter baskets over her arm, running around the Howard Johnson pool at 4:00 a.m."

TAKE NOTE

Bev Hedrick always begins her Easter Hunt with a scavenger hunt for the traditional baskets. Notes in the dryer lead to notes in the cereal box which lead to notes and more notes, leading finally to the Easter baskets. The baskets are great, but in the Hedrick family the notes are the memory-makers.

Frances Goldwasser

JEWISH HOLIDAYS

Jewish holidays bring families together to celebrate the history and the rituals of the Hebrew people. The traditions of the faith are a binding source of strength and a connective link from generation to generation.

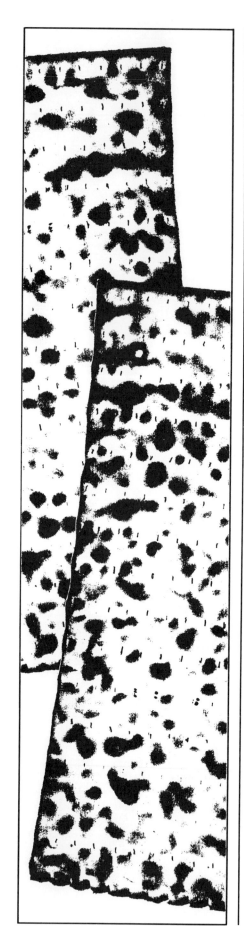

ROSH HASHANAH AND YOM KIPPUR

The New Year or High Holy Days are the most faithfully observed of all Jewish days. Rosh Hashanah is a time to pray that your name will be written in the Book of Life for the coming year. It is followed by Yom Kippur, a day of fasting and prayer to be forgiven for the sins of the past year. In many families this is also a time to eat honey together in hopes of sharing a sweet year.

Opera star Roberta Peters fasts all day on Yom Kippur. It is her tradition to sing "The Twenty-third Psalm" and "They Are at Peace" for the congregation in her synagogue during the closing holiday service.

The Jewish Holidays are observed from sundown to sundown. After Yom Kippur, the breaking of the fast is a family time. The family of Nathanson breaks fast with traditional honey for a sweet year and their favorite breakfast foods. Said one son, "Thinking about our sundown breakfast gets me through the day."

PASSOVER

The Passover is the Jewish festival of freedom which celebrates the exodus of the Israelites from Egypt. Families joyously celebrate the Passover at home with a feast called the Seder. It includes the traditional reading of the Passover story, singing, and participation by all ages. "Every family observes the Seder in its own way," says Trudy Baker. "At our house, the Seder is like being in a play. I am the youngest and my part of the ritual is to ask the four questions about the meaning of the holiday."

Margie Schorr spent a semester at Oxford under the auspices of the Experiment in International Living. She had a Seder for twenty young people, only five of whom were Jewish. The Seder is one of the oldest of all continuing traditions, and people of many faiths enjoy sharing this historical ritual. The Last Supper was a Seder.

The large New York family of Rose celebrates with an annual Black

Tie Seder. The holiday is an important one, and everyone dresses for the occasion.

During the Passover holiday no bread is eaten. Unleavened bread, matzo, is eaten to symbolize the way the exiles lived and ate in the desert. Shoshona Silberman in *The Jewish Family Life* suggests a popcorn party before Passover. The house is then cleaned of all unleavened bread. This custom is probably the basis of spring cleaning!

HANUKKAH

Hanukkah is the festival of lights. Festive candles are lighted on each of eight nights. "We have a menorah for each person in the family; it avoids arguments and adds a touch of splendor to our celebration," says Shoshona Silberman in *The Jewish Family Life*.

Says author Judith Viorst,

> My children have clearly come to find value in lighting the eight-day candles. They all know the prayers, which they take turns repeating each night. And, thugs though they are, they gather around the menorah, combed and washed, neat and even polite, reciting the words that mark the rededication of the Temple by Judas Maccabaeus. Last December, the family was out-of-town for the holiday. They asked to take the menorah with them so they could continue the ritual at the home of their hosts. They wished to do this not because they are especially devout, but because this tradition gives them something they need. It gives them a gratifying sense of their Jewish identity, as does our Passover rite, where we sit at the table with friends, sharing the tale of the Exodus — and my matzo balls.

HIGH LIFE

Mae Shafter Rockland gives her children coins to symbolize the coining of money by the Maccabees after they achieved independence from the Syrian-Greeks in 164 B.C. The original Hanukkah gift was "Hanukkah gelt coins." "It is my custom to give them one penny on the first night, two on the second, etc., so that by the end of the week they have the grand sum of thirty-six cents. This has a nice symbolic quality because thirty-six is twice eighteen, which is also represented by the Hebrew world 'High' meaning 'Life.'"

EVERYDAY TRADITIONS

Births, birthdays, weddings, funerals, religious and national holidays can account for about nineteen days a year. That leaves 346 "leftover" days to deal with, and we all know what leftovers can be like without a little imagination. Spice up leftovers with your own recipe for special home-grown traditions. Some of the most tempting memories can be made with scraps of family times, mini-holidays, C.A.R.E. packages, and ideas for "old family dears."

FAMILY TIME

We invest in fitness, beauty, and business. Families deserve equal time. This is no small task. With everyone in the family merrily racing down his separate path of activities, it takes a mastermind and a math major to find a common-denominator interest and a time to fit it in. If the family is always busy, make family time a scheduled calendar appointment. Mark it "A Date with Dynasty."

MON **22**

*Evening:
Our Time!*

INVESTING TIME IN FAMILY PAYS OFF!

The Mormons (Church of Jesus Christ of Latter Day Saints) observe a weekly Family Home Evening. It is a time set aside to be in touch and connected with the family.

The Alterman family has a traditional Sabbath dinner every Friday night. Each week, there is the same loving meal and blessing and the family is again gathered. Friends are always welcomed. The grandparents get to see the clan, friends enjoy the family closeness, and as twenty-year-old grandson Louis Franco remarked, "I like it. No matter what the week brings, there is Shabbos. You can count on it."

SECRET SUPPER

Jay Schvaneveldt, sociologist at Utah State University, tells about a family's "Secret Supper Night." In this Utah family, a slip of paper is drawn from a hat. Each person is responsible for one course of the meal. The family members shop separately and cook together, still trying to keep their contribution a surprise. "You should see us all cooking and laughing, trying to keep what we're making a secret until it's served," one daughter says. "It may not be our best meal, but it's the one we most enjoy."

LIGHT UP YOUR LIFE

Another family has a ritual of lighting the candles at the table only when the whole family is together. "When the lights have been dimmed for several nights in a row, everyone senses the need to gather for meal time."

IT'S A DATE

Rabbi Alvin Sugarman, like many people today, leads a very fragmented life with many demands on his time. He feels that family time is a priority. He marks specific time on his calendar for his wife Barbara and for each of his daughters. These times are "our" time and as important to him as the calls of the congregation and the community. No matter what the activity, this is their time to be together, to appreciate and celebrate their relationship.

DRIVE TIME

Interior designer Renee Joel "meets" for lunch with her husband or with one of her three kids, ages 18, 21, and 24. "In the old days, 'family time' was drive-time with them. There were no carpools to activities like Connie's tap-dancing or the boys' swim team practice, so I always drove them. The time we spent to-ing and fro-ing, we really spent together."

A REVOLUTIONARY OLD IDEA

Family Time is a project sponsored by the Million Dollar Round Table, an insurance sales organization. The organization promotes investing time in your family as a revolutionary old idea. The following are some ideas for family-time activities.

★ Develop a Family Service Project. Do leaf raking for an elderly neighbor. Work for a political campaign. Do cookie baking regularly for a hospital or college student. Take on an ecology project; check with Keep America Beautiful in your area and agree to clean up the bank of a stream or a park site in your area.

★ Go to a movie or watch a T.V. show together and discuss it afterwards.

★ Create a Music Night. Each family member chooses and shares his music from hard rock to swing, jazz, or the classics. Explore unfamiliar or favored music together. Check-out records from the library.

★ Make It Note Night. Supply stationery, envelopes, and stamps, and gather with snacks and drinks for all. Make a list of people to ''note.'' Everyone writes a brief news note to each. All are enclosed in appropriate envelopes and mailed. Tape-record some letters. Fun to give and great to receive!

★ Try a Family Night Out Adventure. Take the whole crowd somewhere on a city bus, have a theater night, try a family camping trip.

★ Do Family Exercises Together. Each person shares the responsibility for leading the fun and fitness activities. Jump rope together. Have a race to see who can pick up the most pebbles or marbles with his toes in a minute. The family's laughing place usually gets the greatest workout.

★ Share a Skills Exchange Program. The child teaches a loop-to-loop yo-yo trick or gives a how-to tip for playing video games. Parent teaches how to change a tire or sew on buttons. Age and stage determines the projects. Each shares the agony of ineptness and the ecstasy of expertise.

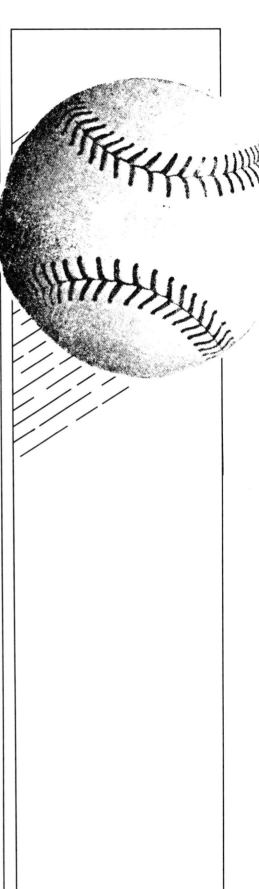

"IF THE TRADITION FITS"

Judith Viorst is a poet and a writer. She greatly admires the tradition of her friends the Martins. On most Sundays, they have a tea and a poetry recitation. The parents, son, and daughter prepare and recite a poem. There is real pride in learning and fun in being able to "strut your stuff" before an appreciative audience. Shakespeare, Shelly, and Silverstein are among the poets.

This tradition, after a few oblique attempts, was not a hit with the three Viorst sons. For them, the weekly spring ritual is a Sunday softball game, played mostly by five or six families of fathers and their sons. (Women *are* invited.) Companionship, not competitiveness, is the goal. "I like it," said middle son Nickolas, "because it's fun to get together and play." "And because it's permanent," he added.

DYNASTY

Some family time leads to big business. It's exciting and rewarding for young people to grow up knowing about the work their parents do. Time spent together recreates the old tradition of apprenticeship. A business learned "at your father's/mother's knee" not only passes along the skills of the trade, but also the passion and enthusiasm for doing it.

Leonard and Ronald Lauder of Estee Lauder Cosmetics, Harold Uris of Uris Building Corporation, and Doris Mattus, daughter of the creators of Häagen-Dazs Ice Cream, are among the many young apprentices who spent afternoons, weekends, and vacations working in the family business. "I was born in an ice cream freezer," said Doris Mattus. "The family business was the dinner table conversation," said another. Growing up learning every position in the family enterprise led Harold Uris to add, "I never thought of going into another business."

Nearly all dynasties are old. Start a new one. Become a family patriarch/matriarch.

LITTLE THINGS
MEAN A LOT

Courtesy, Attention, Recognition, and a little Effort spell C.A.R.E. to lovers, children, and old dears. It's the little things of life that build self-esteem and relationships. Send C.A.R.E. packages regularly.

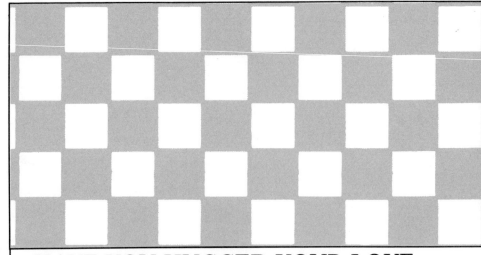

HAVE YOU HUGGED YOUR LOVE, HUSBAND/WIFE/KID/MOM/DAD TODAY?

Author and radio commentator Elmo Ellis described the enthusiastic greetings dogs give. They come running to the door with their tails wagging to say hello and to be petted. The point he was making was the importance of a cheerful greeting and the return of an enthusiastic hug. They show that both parties care.

Stan Brody, chemical engineer and single father of four, ages 3-7, appreciates his family's "tail-wagging" greeting. "All the children wait for me by the door, and they gang up on me. It's such an expression of love," he says as he squeezes each one.

COMMUNICATION WITHOUT HUMILIATION

Public criticism is embarrassing. Silence, with a signal, is golden and gets the point across. Helen and Bill Savitt use the word "governor" as a signal if they wish the other to change the subject.

The Thomas family whistles to locate each other in a public place. Mother whistles, another family member hears it and whistles back. "It may take two or three tries, but it's better than hearing 'Rachel' shouted across a department store floor," says sister Rachel.

One sports-minded family instituted arm signals to indicate a foul. They provide ways to communicate silent disapproval over long distances. A parent can stand on a far hill, hold up three fingers slowly, one at a time, and then give the thumb a quick jerk to the side. The kid knows that if he doesn't move it, he's OUT. These and other signals are effective, especially if a penalty is consistently implemented for noncompliance. This is creative discipline of the *Tough Love* variety. Says the youngest in this clan, "I'm fifteen years old, and if my mom or dad puts up one finger, I've known (since I was three) that she or he means it. It's a conditioned reflex, I guess."

The same family has a sign for when you get it "right." For instance, when you shake hands with one of their friends and make eye contact, they put both hands down by their sides. Thankfully, they don't raise them and yell, "Touchdown."

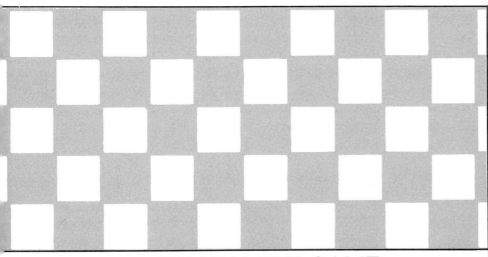

THE FAMILY GAME

Fredelle Maynard, in her book, *Guiding Your Child to a More Creative Life,* describes a game that was the favorite of her children when they were very young:

> Animal Farm was a family invention; we played in on a Candyland board redecorated with pasted-on pictures, so that forfeits and goals corresponded to events in our daily lives. Good squares were "Birthday Party," "School Picnics"; bad squares were labeled "Take out garbage," "You forgot to make your bed. Go back 5." The end of the game was a trip to our favorite circus-zoo. We played the game updating the names and cards, and then at age 10 Rona protested, "This is babyish." Joyce defended it with, "I love Animal Farm. It gives me WFF (Warm Family Feelings).

BED TIME RITUALS ARE REASSURING TO THE VERY YOUNG ... AND YOUNG AT HEART

★ Bedtime is a good time for a recitation of "What are we going to do tomorrow?" The very sameness of the answer is comforting to small children, says sociologist Jay Schvaneveldt.

★ A bedtime back rub is comforting to all ages, according to wife, mother, and masseuse Debbi Tavis.

★ Milk and cookies is a family tradition adopted by Tom and Jane Tracy's family. They were introduced to this custom at the Greenbriar Hotel, where it is an evening courtesy for all guests.

Many families have a bedtime snack. Cookies, ice cream, milk, or even a hot toddy send people to bed with a comfy feeling. So do words like "Can I bring you something?", "It's my turn to get the teaparty tonight," or "What would you like?"

★ One family adopted the Pre-Bedtime Reading Method. "We gave each child the choice of reading for thirty minutes after bedtime or 'Lights Out.' Most kids would rather read the Yellow Pages than to put out the lights ... Reading was a habit — the worse it got, the better it was!"

Joey

168

CHARITY BEGINS AT HOME

Doing for others is a lesson learned early. Milton Wolf, U.S. Ambassador to Austria (1977-80) and the host of the Salt II summit meeting in Vienna, grew up with very limited means. "I did not consider myself poor. There was always a poor box in the kitchen. If you had some pennies, you dropped them in. As a young man, I was aware that there were greater needs than my own."

INSTANT I LOVE YOU'S

Twelve things to do with or for someone you love that take less than twelve minutes.

★ Send someone in the family a hometown postcard. Everyone likes to get mail, especially children.

★ Go on a penny hike. Flip a coin at every corner. If it's heads, go left; tails, turn right.

★ Display shells, rocks, or other finds from nature walks and arts and crafts projects on a prominent coffee table. It's a good feeling to see your work in an important place. DAKS instant plastic frames add recognition to children's art work.

★ Go to a discount store, arcade, or airport together and take crazy pictures in the photo machine. Frame them elaborately.

★ Write "I Love You" on the mirror in lipstick or shaving cream. No one minds how long it stays.

★ Share the tricks and the trivia of your youth. Good luck omens inspire good thoughts and fond memories for fellow believers. Give everyone a rabbit's foot key chain. Honk the horn, touch the inside of the roof of the car, and make a wish when a train passes overhead.

★ Serve popcorn for major T.V. viewings.

★ Write "You're Charmin' " on a roll of toilet paper.

★ On a warm night, go outside and count the stars together. Look for the Little Dipper. Listen to the night sounds. Look at nature with a flashlight.

★ Put a flower or plant on the bedside table when someone has the "blahs." Tom Chase sent his eighteen-year-old daughter four helium-filled balloons attached to a mug filled with a can of chicken soup when she had four wisdom teeth pulled.

★ Put a joke in the briefcase, pocketbook, or lunchbox of a loved one. Put this one on the pillow the night before the dentist appointment: "What did the Wolfman eat after he had his teeth filled? ... The dentist!"

★ In the fall, plant a few bulbs in a secret spot in a public park with someone special. Enjoy them together in the spring.

MINI-HOLIDAYS

"CELEBRATE GOOD TIMES — COME ON.
THERE'S A PARTY GOIN' ON RIGHT HERE,
A CELEBRATION,
TO LAST THROUGHOUT THE YEAR."
— Kool and the Gang

Mini-holidays make the ordinary days extraordinary. Running in a race, passing a tough course, learning to tie your shoes, or coming home from a business trip are all events worthy of a celebration. Nine out of ten who have tried it agree that celebrating regularly gives amazing relief to slow-moving days.

CELEBRATE

THE TOOTH FAIRY TRADITION

The tooth fairy has weird ways at some homes. In one family the missing tooth is put into an envelope and put under the pillow. The Tooth Fairy replaces the envelope containing the tooth with an identical envelope containing the money. The hassle of hunting for the tiny tooth is gone and the pay-off is mysteriously in place.

New mother Debby Hamilton grew up with a Tooth Fairy who advertised good dental care. She always left new toothbrushes and toothpaste.

THE DAY THAT BRACES COME OFF

A special day that should be observed with a special menu. Corn on the cob, barbecued ribs, and bubble gum are great starters for teeth without tin.

MISSING TWO FRONT TEETH

Losing your two front teeth is a tradition. One family marked this milestone with a photograph of their daughter and used it as their Christmas card. When the daughter's daughter was at this stage, she recreated the original photograph and presented both "toothless wonders" photos to her mother as a gift.

1955

COLLEGE DEPARTURES

The prospects of college cafeteria cuisine merit a farewell banquet of favorite family foods. When someone in their household leaves for college, one family has a special ritual. Each child moves over one chair. The next oldest takes over the chair of the oldest. It is a family rite of passage.

Bick Cardwell celebrated a similar rite when his sister married and moved away. He toasted her with this poem: "When my sister married, she got a groom. I thought it was great 'cuz I got her room."

VACATION CELEBRATIONS

Vacations are a tradition. Broadcaster Fred Barber and his wife Evelyn go to the same beach every year. Just the sight of the site gives them instant R and R.

The Chambers family takes long trips out West. When the children were small and there was too much togetherness in the car, the family would stop at a cafeteria for lunch. The parents would eat at one table, kids at another. But if the togetherness had been too terrific, everyone would eat at a separate table.

Family-planning expert Dr. Bob Hatcher's family has a D.O.D. for all family trips. One child is elected Director of Departure and it is his duty to pack the car, plan the picnic, provide pillows, blankets, and games, and assign who sits next to whom. "I can't imagine starting a trip without our D.O.D.," added educator and mother Carolyn Hatcher.

1980

CELEBRATE FAMILY FIRSTS

Make a big splash for the first back dive of the summer, the first one to clean out the garage, or the first one to finish the summer reading list. Cake and ice cream with candles is the treat.

A California woman gives a party every year to celebrate the first bloom of her flowering peach tree. The tree is lit with miniature white Christmas tree lights and a wonderful celebration follows.

WELCOME HOME BANNERS

Announce an arrival. Make an Instant Banner by cutting a pillowcase at the sides. Spray paint the word ''Welcome.'' Use it for loved ones returning from business, camp, or college trips. Enhance the celebration of any arrival with a trip to the bus or plane with the family car loaded with balloons and a basket of snacks and cold drinks for the weary traveler.

Faith Brunson and other book personalities greeted author Joan Walsh Anglund at the airport carrying welcoming placards and dressed in costumes like the characters in her books.

ELECTION NIGHT PARTIES

Make the event special by having all of the campaign workers sign one of the banners as a gift to the candidate. If you're interested in politics, involve your kids. They will see how the process works and then perhaps you can celebrate their candidacy in a school election.

RETIREMENT

A great time for a family fete. One family had T-shirts made for the whole family that said, ''Grandpop Power.''

HAVE A PROMOTION COMMOTION

Any raise or change of position is an excuse for flowers or festival. The wife of an attorney proudly threw a Legal Eagle Party and opened the bar when her husband passed the Bar.

In another city a proud pop gave his daughter a party with an invitation that proclaimed, "My Daughter, the Doctor."

INSTITUTE A
ROAD RUNNERS RITUAL

Nancy and Skip Elsas attend an annual After-the-Peachtree-Road-Race Party on the Fourth of July. Their English hosts serve a breakfast of strawberries and cream to friends. Another spectator-spouse created a special souvenir by framing her finisher's T-shirt from the same race.

BACK TO SCHOOL BREAKFAST

One mother started a Back to School ritual. She invited four or five first-graders for breakfast on the first day of school so her child could walk into class with some buddies. The Back to School breakfast became an annual tradition lasting through high school.

T.G.I.G.

In 1979 Debby First went through a year of chemotherapy after a cancer operation. At the end of the year, she was doing fine and her hair was growing back. She and her husband Bob had a party to thank their friends and family who had been so supportive. The invitation was a T.G.I.G. T-shirt inviting everyone to celebrate T.G.I.G. — Thank God It's Growing!

175

176

CELEBRATE
BY HAVING A PICNIC

Cut down on dinner doldrums. Change the pace with a change of place. If you picnic regularly, it becomes a tradition. Columnist Celestine Sibley loves the tradition of picnicking. "Somehow the pleasure in eating food anywhere but under a roof at home infected my mother and was passed on to me."

Here are pointers on picnic places, plans, and paraphernalia.

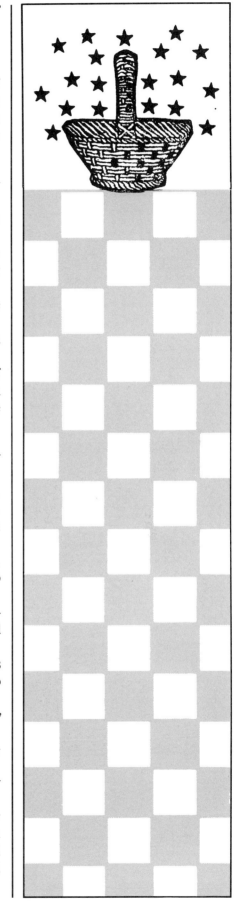

PLACES

★ Picnic where the action is: Watch a tennis match, a Little League game, a horse show, or a track meet.

★ Sup by a stream. Keep your eyes open for a cool brook and return later for a picnic. A picnic and a wade-in are a great prize (bribe) for a "quiet" weekend ride.

★ Picnic at a construction site. Earthmovers and building cranes are awesome entertainment.

★ Take your tickets and your taskets to a summer concert. (This is a wonderful introduction for reluctant symphony-goers.)

★ Try an old cemetery for a picnic with a past. Bring a large sheet of newsprint and a crayon and do a rubbing. Place the paper on a favorite tombstone and rub the crayon on the paper to pick up the design and inscription. Frame it.

★ Choose a spot at the zoo and let the animals watch you.

PLANS

★ *Pique-nique* is a French word. Pick up a French loaf, some cheese, fruit, wine, and a whole chicken from the grocery store rotisserie. Pick, or pick up, some flowers for the basket and, voilà, un pique-nique! Definitely preferable to a McPicnic.

★ Breakfast Alfresco. Julia Shivers serves juice, croissants, butter, preserves, and cafe au lait in her gazebo (patio or porch will do) to start many a day.

★ Fireside Picnics. Candlelight or firelight makes for wonderful fireside chats. They add life to winter evenings or rainy days. Add music and marshmallows and it's a real memory-maker.

★ Tailgate Picnics. Station wagon tailgates can serve a sumptuous buffet, complete with silver and caviar. These picnics add style to stadium parking lots in football season.

★ Barbecue. Anything cooked outside tastes better. *Roughing It Easy* by Dian Thomas, Warner Books, has unique ideas for cookouts

★ Hobo Picnics. Send your hobos outside with a sack supper, for your privacy and theirs.

PARAPHERNALIA

A picnic basket is a wonderful gift for families. Give one to your family first. Baskets include a blanket or quilt, tin plates (lightweight and lovely), giant picnic napkins (use wash-and-wear fabric pinked around the edges), two chunky candles, and wine glasses. Keep it always ready; all that's needed are flowers and food.

PROSPECTING
THE
GOLDEN YEARS

Restore the traditions of "The Golden Years." Take care of your old dears today. Set an example and establish a tradition that, hopefully, your youngsters will follow.

MILE STONES

MARCH 9, 1901

ADVANCE 1

BIG CITY LIFE

1919

JUST VISITING

WILD OATS

GO BACK 2

TRUE LOVE

1938

MOVE 3

I HOPE SEVENTY-FIVE IS FUN WHEN I GET THERE!

The "Today Show" featured a story about Bob McClain, a department store manager in his thirties, who chucked his position to become a handyman. Not only did he fix and repair things for his customers, especially older ones, but he also listened to their tales. His attention broke the silence that engulfed many of their lives.

When the interviewer asked him how he would feel about getting to be seventy-five, he was taken aback for a minute and then he grinned and said, "Well, if there are more guys like me around, then I think it would be fine."

The respect for age shouldn't get lost in the shuffle of a youth-oriented culture. If we're lucky, we'll all make it to this ripe old spot still wanting attention, needing to feel a sense of importance, and eager for a shot of T.L.C. along with our daily pile of pills.

THAT OLD FEELING

One thoughtful daughter answered requests about gifts for her mother with the suggestion that they be "a little sexy." "You never get over the feeling of wanting to be attractive." The granddaughter solved her problem by going to a prep (translated traditional) shop and buying her grandmother a blouse. The card read, "Grandma is a Preppie."

Other grandmother gift ideas include: the newest hot color in blouses, a lacy half-slip, a facial, a personal color analysis, or a biography of her favorite movie star, even though, as one grandmother said, "I buried it in the back yard AFTER I finished it."

Grandfathers need the same attention. Try these suggestions:

★ Designer chic appeals to all ages. The double Gucci G's can represent Great Gramps/Great Guy or Gal.
★ A cassette-player so you can send each other tapes instead of letters.
★ A dozen Golden Balloons delivered at dinner in the nursing home for no special reason.

AS THE WORLD TURNS

Nursing home visits can be a nuisance. The following solution to this problem required only a small amount of Rachel Hugh's time. "When I'd visit my husband's grandmother in the nursing home, the visits were a real struggle. She was nearly ninety, and, being in-laws, we had little in common and little shared history. The Soaps were the solution.

"I started watching her Soap whenever I could. Instantly, we knew people in common and could discuss the characters and their problems as if they had been our lifelong friends. The newspaper ran a weekly update on the Soaps and when I couldn't view, I'd read to catch up. Our visits improved immediately. We could even get into big discussions over the phone. We both loved hating Jessica!"

THIS IS YOUR LIFE

Taking care of older stepparents can be a problem unless you turn it into a plus. One stepdaughter had a ball and learned firsthand, fabulous history about her "wicked stepfather," whom she adored, when she asked him to write his biography for her family and his.

After my mother died I wanted to spend some time with him and the biography gave us a joint project. We'd meet for lunch now and then as the chapters began to come. I was the editor. I learned so much about his life that I would never have touched on in general conversation.

After about four or five years the project was complete. The pages were typed, xeroxed, and then bound by a local bindery (see Yellow Pages) for under thirty dollars a book. He ordered three books which were beautifully leather bound in his favorite color. The title was done in gold lettering.

My favorite part of the project was hearing his comment at the conclusion of his life story. "You know, I've come to find that it's been a darn good life and I wouldn't have missed a minute of it."

A MUTUAL ADOPTION

Pedodontist and golfer David Epstein came to Hartford, Connecticut, from Michigan. He met senior citizen Bill Savitt on the golf course. His young family needed some in-town grandparents and the Savitts' children were grown and in other states. "We had a mutual need and have developed a mutual interest, love, and respect for each other's life."

THE GAME OF LIFE

Juliet Chase wanted a unique present for her father, so she created the Game of Life. She took an old board game and covered the board labels with her father's milestones: his birthdate, school, jobs, honors, wedding, grandchildren, and favorite sayings and traditions. There were bonus squares that read, "First job at the bank," "First child born," "Received community award," each advancing the player three to five squares. There were also penalty squares. "College check bounces," "Appendix out," or "Watching football on T.V." sent the player back three spaces. "The family learned about Dad, and he hit the memory jackpot with every roll of the dice."

HOT WHEELS

1940

MOVE 3 SPACES

LIABILITY

GO BACK 6 SPACES

ASSET

1941, 1943

ADVANCE 1 SPACE

FLY UNITED

FAMILY HOLIDAYS

ADVANCE 2 SPACES

FAVORITE FOODS

Food is at the heart of almost every celebration for which family and friends gather. The sights, smells, and tastes of favorite recipes excite memories faster than any other experience.

The sweet smell of a butter-rich pound cake, the heady aroma of sauteed bacon and onions, or even the rank odor of cabbage or shrimp cooking often means that regional, ethnic, or personal food traditions are in the making. Families and friends gather around the table, the picnic cloth, the barbecue grill, the clambake, but mostly around the kitchen stove to share old times or create new culinary memories.

There can be no book on traditions without a sampling of old-favorite recipes. Each of these recipes has a tale to tell and is very much a part of a tradition. Many of them have been handed down, changed, modified, and simplified. Convenience substitutes have been included. Most of the cooks have made these recipes for years with a "pinch of this, lots of that, or a bunch of this." They record their recipes in this fashion, but with prompting have included measurable amounts. The results are old favorites the way their friends and family enjoy them.

From the wood-burning stove to the microwave, the American melting pot continues to simmer. Enjoy these flavorful traditions!

EGGNOG

In 1931 Ruth and Jack Adams married and moved to New York. They wanted her family's recipe for eggnog to celebrate their first Christmas together. Ruth wrote home for the recipe and received this wire in return. It was during Prohibition and neither whiskey nor eggnog was supposed to be in speakeasys much less in telegrams, so the ingredients were altered. Translate "one tablespoon any flavoring" to read "one jigger whiskey" and you've got an eggnog that is rich in taste, calories, and tradition.

Holiday Greeting
WESTERN UNION

CCP67 50 NL GTG25 = TAMPA FLO
MR AND MRS J W ADAMS =
    APT 2 F 26 GROVE ST NEWYORK NY =
ALL WISH YOU BOTH VERY MERRY CHRISTMAS RECIPE FOR TEN PEOPLE ONE QUART WHIPPING CREAM EIGHTEEN EGGS ONE TABLESPOON SUGAR AND ONE TABLESPOON ANY FLAVORING TO EACH EGG SECRET IS HAVING YOLKS BEATEN WELL THEN BEAT IN SUGAR THEN FLAVORING NEXT FOLD IN STIFFLY WHIPPED WHITES THEN STIFFLY WHIPPED CREAM THE FAMILY

1 qt. whipping cream
18 eggs
1 Tbs. sugar per egg
1 jigger whiskey per egg

Separate egg yolks and whites. The secret to this recipe is having yolks beaten well.
Beat in sugar and whiskey.
Next, fold in stiffly whipped egg whites and stiffly whipped cream.

GAELIC COFFEE

The annual St. Patrick's Day Parade in New York city is world famous. Savannah, Georgia, also has a great day for Ireland's patron saint and the second largest parade in the nation. The early morning mass at St. John the Baptist Cathedral is followed by breakfast get-togethers sponsored by seven or eight Irish organizations. From 10 to 12 o'clock a city-wide parade takes place. As Father Boland says, "Everyone in Savannah is Irish on St. Patrick's Day."

Bands, bystanders, and celebrities come from everywhere to revel in this tradition. In the evening the Hibernian Society, founded in Savannah in 1821, holds a stag party for 800-900 males. Bill Kehoe, one of the past presidents of the Society, says even a menu of local recipes bears the flavor of the Irish heritage.

¾ c. coffee
2 tsp. brown sugar
1 jigger Irish whiskey
Whipping cream

Whip cream until only slightly thickened. It must be "pourable."
Heat glass with boiling water — an essential step.
Pour out water and fill to ¾ with piping hot coffee.
Add brown sugar and stir well.
Add a minimum of 1 jigger of good Irish Whiskey.
Stir.
Pour cream gently over back of hot spoon to float on top of coffee.
(This recipe is for 1 serving.)

UNGSPANKAKA

Minnesota was settled by many Swedish families whose contributions include their traditions and old family recipes.

Julie and Bill Robertson grew up enjoying Ungspankaka, a traditional New Year's Day recipe. It is an egg-pancake cut into squares and served with syrup. "It is a meal in itself and is so good that we eat it all year," says Julie.

3 eggs
2 c. milk
1 tsp. salt
⅔ c. flour
2 Tbsp. sugar
6 strips bacon

Fry bacon and break into pieces.
Melt pat of butter in an 8″ square cake pan and coat pan.
Beat eggs, milk, salt.
Add flour and sugar and mix well.
Pour in batter and add bacon.
Bake at 350° about 35 minutes.
Serves 4. If the recipe is doubled, make in 9″ × 13″ pan.
It will have to bake a little longer if doubled, about 40-45 minutes.
It should puff up and be golden brown.
Cut in squares and serve with syrup.
Serves 4.

CHICKEN LIVER

The specialty of the house is often a closely held secret. The secret of one cook's wonderful Chopped Chicken Liver is that she *buys* it at the Snack and Shop Delicatessen in Atlanta, Georgia. The real cook is Renee Feldman, who carries on her mother-in-law's traditional recipe. Says Renee, "If you like to make the recipe a little fancy, add a bit of cognac, press the liver into a decorative mold, and call it pate."

2 lbs. calves liver cut thick
8 large eggs (hard boiled)
1 sweet onion
4 Tbs. rendered chicken fat or substitute "Schmaltz-e-dige" made by Carmel Kosher
1 Tbs. mayonnaise
Salt and pepper to taste

Broil the liver until cooked through, but not dry.
Trim hard edges and any sinew.
Cut into chunks.
Put through coarse grinder (do not puree in processor).
Grind eggs and onions in same way.
Blend all together with melted fat, salt and pepper, and a little of the mayonnaise to blend.
Let chill.

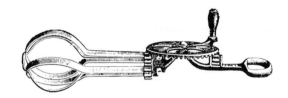

WILD DUCK

Career consultant Betsy Baker grew up near Stuttgart, Arkansas, one of the duck-hunting capitals of the world. ''It was not unusual to see the boys of Pine Bluff High School arrive in their knee-high rubber boots with wild ducks tied to the top of their cars to begin class after an early morning hunt in the rice paddies. Stuttgart was the scene of many a good time and good wild duck eating feasts. Each family had its own special recipe.''

2 cleaned wild ducks
Salt and pepper
Garlic powder
1 quartered apple per duck
1 chopped onion per duck
2 chopped celery stalks per duck
1 bay leaf per duck
4 strips bacon
4 lemon slices
8-10 cans consomme

Season birds inside and out with salt, pepper, and garlic powder.
Stuff with apple, onion, celery, and bay leaf.
Place in a large roaster and add two strips of bacon and two slices lemon per duck.
Pour consomme in roaster (not over birds) and cover half the birds.
Bake for 3½ hours, covered, at 300°-325° until tender.
Continue to add consomme to keep birds moistened.
Halve ducks and prepare sauce.

SAUCE

2 Tbs. flour to thicken
1½ c. consomme
1 c. red wine
1 c. whipping cream

To about 1½ cups consomme that has been cooked in pan, add enough flour to thicken.
Add red wine and put duck halves in sauce, breast side down, and baste.
Simmer on stove top for about an hour, basting frequently.
Before serving, add cream.

GOURMET STEAK

When chef Yvette Greune came to America from Dortmund, West Germany, she had visions of opening her own restaurant. Within a few years, this resourceful young woman opened the Old Vinings Inn to gourmet acclaim. Her recipes are imaginative and delicious and include some old family favorites.

1 medium sliced onion
1 sliced banana
2 8-10 oz. strip steaks
4 Tbs. oil
1 tsp. Dijon mustard
½ tsp. curry
3 Tbs. port wine
6 Tbs. vodka
½ tsp. salt
½ c. brown sauce (package kind is O.K.)
4 Tbs. heavy cream
1 Tbs. butter

Heat oil in heavy skillet (iron) and saute onions 2 minutes or until light brown. Set aside.
Season steaks and cook 1 minute each side (in same pan). Set aside. Place onions on stop of steaks and keep warm.
Add mustard and curry and bananas in skillet. Stir and add port and vodka.

Carefully light, then let flames subside.
Add brown sauce, cream, and butter.
Pour over steaks.

LASAGNA

In the Plumeri family no holiday is complete without Josephine Plumeri's lasagna. ''For years the children complained that serving lasagna left little room for the turkey, so one year I gave them a complete turkey dinner without lasagna. Then everyone complained that it really wasn't Thanksgiving the way they liked it.''

The Plumeri Tomato Sauce can be used with many other recipes. Make a double recipe and freeze it for future use with chicken, omelettes or spaghetti.

MEATBALLS

1 lb. ground beef
1½ c. Italian flavored bread crumbs
2 eggs
3 Tbs. parmesan cheese
Salt and pepper to taste

Mix ingredients and shape into balls the size of a half dollar. Set aside.
Cut 1 lb. of Italian sausage in 3-inch pieces. Lightly brown. Set aside.

TOMATO SAUCE

1 lb. ground beef
6 6-oz. cans tomato paste
1 large can plum tomatoes
1 clove garlic
3 Tbs. olive oil
1 small bay leaf
Fresh or dried basil
1 tsp. sugar
Salt and pepper to taste

Lightly brown garlic in oil, add ground beef, and saute until pink is gone.
Add tomato paste and tomatoes and saute about 5 minutes.
Add about 12 cans of water, using tomato paste can as measure.
Bring to boil and add meatballs and browned sausage.
Simmer about 1 hour.

RICOTTA FILLING

2 lbs. ricotta cheese
2 eggs
3 Tbs. parmesan cheese
Black pepper, a little salt

Mix all ingredients until smooth

1 lb. shredded mozzarella cheese
1 lb. lasagna noodles cooked according to package directions

To assemble lasagna, remove meatballs and sausage from sauce and keep warm.
Cover bottom of lasagna pan with sauce, place a layer of noodles, layer of ricotta mixture, mozzarella cheese, and sauce and sprinkle with parmesan cheese. Repeat layers until all ingredients are used, ending with ricotta mixture and sauce. Cover with foil and bake in 350° pre-heated oven for about 30 minutes. Let stand about 5 minutes and then remove foil. Cut in serving portions. Serve with extra cheese and sauce along with sausage and meatballs.
Served with a salad, Italian crusty bread, and rose wine for a very satisfying meal. Serves about 10 for main course or more as a side dish.
Helpful hints: The above sauce is a base for other Italian dishes, such as Eggplant Parmesan, Veal and Peppers, omelettes, and Italian vegetables, like zucchini, so double the recipe and freeze.
The meatballs and sausage can be used for sandwiches on hard rolls for lunch or a light supper.

185

ENCHILADAS

Carolyn Wilson was a student at Southern Methodist University in Dallas when she was introduced to the tradition of eating "Tex-Mex," Texas-Mexican food. When she graduated and moved back home, she craved the Tex-Mex treats, so friends began to send her recipes to tide her over until she could get back to Texas and the "real thing." The following recipes will help satisfy food fits brought on by prolonged absences from chili and enchiladas. Her family is now hooked on the tradition. Carolyn adds, "You can't beat it for cooking for a crowd of kids."

1 lb. grated cheddar cheese
2-3 chopped onions
2 lbs. hamburger meat
2 cloves garlic, minced
5 cans chili (without beans)
18-30 frozen or canned tortillas
Salt, pepper, and tabasco sauce to taste

Cook hamburger meat, 1 chopped onion, and garlic seasoned with salt, pepper, and tabasco.
Drain grease and put meat in bowl.
Sit down with all ingredients in front of you and get ready to roll.
Use loaf pans to cook in.
Put a little meat, cheese, onion, and heated chili in a tortilla and roll it up.
After the pan is filled, sprinkle onions and any left-over meat, chili, and cheese (in this order only) on the top.
Be sure to use enough chili so that enchiladas do not stick and are not dry.
Cook until all ingredients are thoroughly heated, about 1 hour at 300°.
Serves 8-10, allowing 2-3 enchiladas per person.

CHILI

It is traditional to have a pot boiling on Halloween. Advertising director Anne Goodsell's pot is her Crock Pot and she keeps it simmering all day with chili to accommodate the phantom hordes of family, trick-or-treaters, or grown-ups who appear later in the evening with hungry looks beneath their masks. Chili, slaw, jalapeno, and cornbread are ready and waiting for all those spooks and clowns who go bump in the night.

1 lb. ground chuck
1 can tomatoes
1 medium onion, chopped
1 green pepper, chopped
5 or 6 jalapeno slices, minced
1½ pkg. French's Chili-o seasoning (only brand)
1 tsp. pepper
Salt only if needed
1 can chili beans in sauce

Brown chuck, onion, pepper together.
Sprinkle seasonings on top and stir.
Puree tomatoes in food processor and add jalapenos.
Add beans, adjust seasonings, and crock all day.
This recipe serves 4.
For a crowd, increase the proportions to 5 times the chuck and 4 times the rest.
For a large crowd, it is a good idea to have rice available.

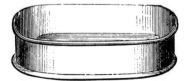

EASTER MENU

The Meek family owned a large ranch in what is now most of downtown Haywood, California. The family home has been preserved and is now a state recreation area. Grandmother Meek, who lived there, passed down the recipes for her favorite Easter meal to her granddaughter, Barbara Stelling.

BOILED MUTTON WITH CAPER SAUCE

6-7 lb. leg of lamb (must be American lamb)
1 large onion
2 cloves
½ lemon, sliced
4-5 sprigs celery tops
7-8 sprigs parsley
2 bay leaves

Place lamb in a large kettle. May need to have butcher cut leg in half to fit pot.
Add remaining ingredients and cover with boiling water.
Return to boil, simmer 10 minutes, and skim top.
Season with salt and pepper to taste.
Cover and simmer until tender, about 30 minutes to the pound.
Remove meat to a large platter, slice and keep warm.
Cover with caper sauce, garnish with watercress, and serve with rice and glazed spring carrots.
Serves 8-10.

CAPER SAUCE

4 Tbs. butter
4 Tbs. flour
3 c. liquid from boiled lamb (Skim off all fat)
3-4 thin slices lemon
1 Tbs. dry mustard
1 bottle whole small capers (Juice included)
2 Tbs. butter (optional)

Make roux of butter and flour.
Gradually add hot stock, stirring well.
Cook and stir until smooth.
Add remaining ingredients.
Season with salt and pepper to taste.
For richer sauce add remaining butter.

CRAB CASSEROLE

Jane Turner, wife of sportsman and broadcaster Ted Turner, leads an exciting life. She lives on a 5,000-acre plantation in South Carolina with her family. They love the sea, sailing, and seafood. One of the Turner's favorite recipes is Jane's creation of Crab Casserole.

1 lb. crabmeat
1 lb. small shrimp, cooked and peeled
½ c. chopped bell pepper
1 medium chopped onion
4 hard boiled eggs, chopped
¾ c. chopped celery
1 can cream of mushroom soup
1 c. mayonnaise
1 small pkg. Pepperidge Farm herb stuffing
1½ tsp. worcestershire sauce
½ tsp. salt
¼ tsp. pepper

Mix all ingredients together.
Bake uncovered in buttered pyrex dish (13 × 9 × 2) for 25-30 minutes at 350° until brown.

SHRIMP PILAF

After an evening of conducting a symphony orchestra, Robert Shaw and his wife Caroline entertain their guests at home with a light supper. "Everyone appreciates being served as soon as possible after a performance, especially if they have waited until then for their evening meal. Just before the performance I take the casserole out of the refrigerator. It can be heated quickly in a hot oven as soon as we return. We serve this with a good French Chablis or Muscadet, a Romaine salad, and a fruit sorbet."

6 slices bacon
1 c. uncooked rice
½ stick butter
½ c. finely chopped celery
2 chopped onions
¼ c. chopped green pepper
1 lb. uncooked, cleaned shrimp
Salt and pepper
Worcestershire sauce
Flour
Grated parmesan cheese

Fry bacon crisp.
Drain and add bacon grease to 1¾ c. water.
Add 1 tsp. salt and cook rice in this mixture.
In a separate pan, saute celery, onions, and bell pepper in butter until tender.
Douse shrimp with a generous amount of worcestershire sauce and dredge with salted flour.
Add shrimp to vegetables and cook until flour is no longer gummy.
Season with salt and pepper, add rice mixture, and stir until mixture is quite moist.
Add parmesan cheese to taste, more butter or herbs if you desire.
Add the crumbled bacon.
Place in well-buttered casserole and refrigerate or bake in a very hot oven (400°) until thoroughly heated.
Serves 4 people generously and can be easily doubled or tripled.

SCALLOPED OYSTERS

Gussie Mae Heard has been cooking in the Lawrence Knox household in Thomson, Georgia, for 35 years. Her cooking and her recipes are a tradition in themselves. As Margaret Knox says, "putting a 'Gussie Recipe' into proper cookbook form with specific measurements and prescribed method is as easy as capturing moonbeams or fathoming love. Gussie's extraordinary and totally delectable cooking is based on a pinch of this, a dash of that, and a vast amount of amazing good sense.

"Every year at our traditional Christmas gathering she prepares scalloped oysters. The secret of Gussie's cooking is in using the very basics. Even a near miss with Gussie's scalloped oysters is still a delight to the palate."

1 qt. oysters
1 stack crushed saltine crackers
1 pt. milk or Half and Half
½ c. butter (1 stick)
Salt and pepper

Grease a 2 qt. casserole generously with butter or margarine.
Sprinkle coarsely crushed saltines sparingly on bottom.
Put half of the oysters over saltines. Salt and pepper lightly.
Cover with another layer of saltines and a few dots of butter or margarine.
Make second layer of oysters.
Top with crushed saltines.
Pour enough milk over mixture to moisten thoroughly.
Dot top generously with butter.
Put into pre-heated oven set at 375°.
Cook until mixture is firm, but not dry, and brown on top, about 35-40 minutes.
Serves 6-8.

TURKEY DRESSING

When CBS correspondent Lesley Stahl was dating writer Aaron Lathem, he invited her "home for the holidays" to meet his family. They arrived to find his mother sick in bed. It became Lesley's job to prepare the Christmas dinner, a task she had not previously undertaken. After seventeen long-distance phone calls to her mother in Boston, she did it! "Aaron had to marry me after that," she exclaimed.

Here is the Mother-Daughter recipe for the turkey dressing. There were only four at their Christmas dinner and enough dressing for a multitude.

1 8 oz. box of Ritz crackers
1 pkg. Pepperidge Farm stuffing
¼ lb. butter
1 red pepper, diced
1 green pepper, diced
2 medium onions, finely diced
1-2 grated carrots
4-5 diced celery stalks
4 cans button mushrooms
6 eggs

Saute celery, carrots, peppers, onions, and mushrooms in butter.
Crush crackers, combine with stuffing, and add to vegetables.
Beat eggs and add to the mixture.
Stuff the turkey and bake according to the weight of the turkey.

TOMATO ASPIC

Betty Hudson is Vice-President for Corporate Relations for NBC. During the holiday season, her friends frequently entertain with covered dish celebrations. Over the years, Tomato Aspic has become her standard dish.

1 envelope gelatin
1¾ c. V-8 juice
2 Tbs. lemon juice
2 tsp. worcestershire sauce
1 Tbs. horseradish
½ tsp. salt
Dash of tabasco sauce
1 c. celery, chopped fine
1 green pepper, chopped fine
½ c. chopped pecans
½ c. sliced olives

Soften gelatin in ½ cup of V-8 juice, then dissolve mixture in remainder of V-8 juice which has been brought to a boil.
Add the seasonings.
Stir in celery, pepper, pecans, and olives.
Chill in mold.
Makes 4 cups.

SPANAKOPITA

Spanakopita is a popular Greek spinach pie. For Euterpe Dukakis it is an ever-evolving recipe which is continually changing with the times. Her mother grew her own spinach and made the dough from scratch. At 79, Euterpe has taken some short cuts in keeping with her busy modern life. She spent 1982 campaigning for her son Michael Dukakis's election as governor of Massachusetts.

2 eggs
½ lb. fresh spinach or 2 pkg. frozen leaf spinach
1 small onion or 3 scallions, chopped
2 Tbs. olive oil
½ tsp. salt
½ "generous" lb. feta cheese, crumbled fine
"A little" dill (preferably fresh)
½ lb. phylo (strudel or baklava dough)
½ lb. melted butter

Frozen spinach: Put in refrigerator overnight. Cut in ½-inch squares. Put in a large pan until completely thawed. Squeeze out all liquid.

Fresh spinach: Wash and cut into ½-inch pieces. Sprinkle with salt and let stand 1 hour. Squeeze out all liquid.

Filling: Saute onions in oil. Beat eggs, and add onions and oil, dill, cheese, spinach and salt. Mix thoroughly.

Pie: Preheat oven to 350°. Oil a 13″×9″ pan well. Spread half the phylo layer by layer. Brush each layer with melted butter. Add the filling and top with remaining phylo, again brushing each layer with butter. The top layer should be well-buttered. Turn edges with a knife to seal in filling. Score lightly in 2-inch squares and bake until lightly brown, about 50-60 minutes.

Cool, cut completely, reheat, and serve.

CHARLOTTE RUSSE

Charlotte Russe was one of Dearee Lokey's favorite family recipes. Dearee's real name was Rebecca, but she was called Dear Re or Dearee by her first grandchild. Before that she had also been affectionately known as "Miss Re" or "Misery" by her southern family and friends.

"Dearee" not only made this favorite recipe for family but also took it to friends in the hospital or those who were sick at home. Charlotte Russe is usually made with several teaspoons of sherry, but Dearee made hers with *one* cup of the fortified spirit, which left patients as well as guests "feeling ever so much better."

3-4 egg whites
2 envelopes plain gelatin
¾ c. sugar
1 c. sherry (cook's preference)
1 pt. whipping cream

Mix sugar and wine in a large bowl.

Mix gelatin in ½ cup water which is then placed in a pan of simmering water to dissolve.

Whip egg whites until almost stiff.

Add gelatin mixture to sherry and sugar.

Fold egg whites into mixture, stirring carefully to blend liquids.

Whip cream and fold into mixture, carefully blending to avoid streaks.

Pour this gelatin/mousse mixture into a mold or put into container to take to friends.

Makes 1½-2 quarts or 10-12 servings.

"This will keep well in the refrigerator," Dearee adds. "It never keeps well in my refrigerator though, because the family loves it."

WHITE FRUIT CAKE

The recipe for the famous Claxton fruit cake evolved from a custom started at Tos' Bakery by the ladies of Claxton, Georgia. Each Christmas, these ladies made large fruit cakes. Their ovens did not produce satisfactory results, so they asked Mr. Tos to let them bake their cakes in his large ovens. For a charge of 50¢ the ladies got evenly baked fruit cakes and Mr. Tos recognized the popularity of fruit cakes as a Christmas custom. He started baking his own cakes based on the recipes of his customers. Each customer thought that the original Claxton fruit cake was based on *her* recipe. Mrs. Swinton Burkalter, whose recipe follows, was *sure* it was hers.

2 lbs. white raisins
2 lbs. candied cherries
2 lbs. candied pineapple
1 c. English walnuts, chopped
4 c. pecans, chopped
½ c. sherry
2 Tbs. black walnut extract
1 lb. butter
1 lb. sugar
1 lb. cake flour
9 large eggs

Flour fruit and nutmeats in half of flour.

Use remaining amount in batter.

Cream butter and sugar.

Add eggs slowly, one at a time.

Sift dry ingredients together.

Add flour and sherry alternately.

Add flavoring and fruit.

Bake in a very slow oven 2½ to 3 hours (about 200°).

Cake should be made at least a week before serving.

BLUEBERRY TARTS

Dr. Charles Wright and his family head to Maine and their favorite seafood dinner every summer. Digging the clams and picking the blueberries along the hiking trails add to the pleasure of the lobster feast. The table is spread with oil cloth anchored with a carafe of cold chablis on either end. Corn, in season, is a must. French bread and a tossed green salad can be served, but the chef adds, "If you're serious about lobster, this is quite enough!"

"This blueberry tart is a real tradition for us. It is a variation of a recipe created by our favorite gourmet cook, Samuel Chamberlain, who knew and loved the coast of Maine," adds wife and assistant chef, Edie.

Bake your own favorite short pie pastry to a light golden brown.

Fill crust with fresh blueberries.

Make a syrup of 1 c. currant jelly and 2 Tbs. water.

Spoon the mixture over the blueberries.

Bake tart for 5 minutes in a hot oven before serving.

CELEBRATIONS

The Celebration Book includes ideas from people all over the country. We invite you to share your traditions with us for Celebrations II.

Chambers & Asher
1776 Nancy Creek Bluff, N.W.
Atlanta, Georgia 30327